The Chrome Cowgirl Guide to
THE
MOTORCYCLE LIFE

The Chrome Cowgirl Guide to
THE
MOTORCYCLE LIFE

Sasha Mullins

motorbooks

First published in 2008 by MBI Publishing Company and Motorbooks, an imprint of MBI Publishing Company, 400 First Avenue North, Suite 300, Minneapolis, MN 55401 USA

Motorbooks titles are also available at discounts in bulk quantity for industrial or sales-promotional use. For details write to Special Sales Manager at MBI Publishing Company, 400 First Avenue North, Suite 300, Minneapolis, MN 55401 USA.

To find out more about our books, join us online at www.motorbooks.com.

ISBN-13: 978-0-7603-2922-1

Cover, title page and back cover photos: Sasha Mullins on Tigerlily. *Michele Lanci-Altomare* Leathers courtesy of Icon Go-Go Gear, rideicon.com

Editors: Darwin Holmstrom and Mariam Pourshartari

Design Team
Art Director: Michele Lanci-Altomare
Design Manager: Tom Heffron
Designer: Danielle Smith
Cover Designer: Cindy Samargia Laun
Tigerlily illustrations: Jesse Boldt:

Printed in the USA

ROAD MAP

DEDICATIONS

This book is dedicated to my amazing Chrome Charming, Patrick S. Lassiter. He loves my Chrome Cowgirl free spirit and encourages me to be me and ride off and lasso my dreams. I love you, dude! In loving memory of John F. Mullins, my daddy Poppi! The man of my world.

THANK YOUs
(in no particular order)

Darwin Holmstrom, Michele Lanci-Altomare, Danielle Smith, Zack Miller, Tom Heffron, Nichole Schiele, Ken Fund, Jesse Boldt, the great crew at Motorbooks, Fritz Clapp, Betsy Huelskamp, Jay Allen, Pete Cimasi, Skip MacLeod, John Beymer, Lori Coon, Bob Smith, Rich Travali, Emma, Poppi, Jodi Ray Sorensen, Hillybilly Hero Dave Powell, Malysa Wyse, Chris Maida, Bandit KRB, GypZ Jingles, Jasmine Cain, Pat Lassiter, Tattoo Willie, Dennis Curnette, English Jim, Bean're, Mike Lichter, Darcy Betlach, Sara Liberte, Marla Browning, Brenda Trumbo, and my dear, dear Jesus.

PREFACE

What's that loud roar? Well, it's this book: *The Chrome Cowgirl Guide to the Motorcycle Life.* It's also the craving in your gut for some freedom in the wind. Are you ready to roar through life, wild and free? Everything good happens on a motorcycle. The motorcycle way of life is about letting go and being true. It teaches you how to live a life that is more liberating and more truthful than you've ever known. Riding a two-wheeled freedom machine is about feeling and being fabulous. The act of riding bubbles with positive energy. It is a delicious, intoxicating rush to the soul.

A girl on a motorcycle is a vision of pure cool. Motorcycles resonate deep in the soul of every female, whether she rides, is a passenger, or dreams about riding a motorcycle. Whether you ride or not, this book is for you. Keep it handy for some odd bits of biker chick inspiration anytime you need a dose.

There's a Chrome Cowgirl in every woman, every girl. There's a beautiful female energy inside all of us that just wants to be wild and free like a pioneering cowgirl riding an untamed mustang. That's what it feels like to ride a motorcycle. And on those two wheels . . . well, you create your own path, you forge your own destiny. You let the adventure happen. You go with the flow of the road. Whether you're a racer chick, a motocross

dirty girl, a highway cruisin' mama—that's where you'll find a Chrome Cowgirl heart.

Ever since I was a tiny girl, I wanted to ride a motorcycle. I would dream that I could fly. I imagined that soaring down the highway on a motorcycle would feel like flying, only my wings would be two wheels with a big roar. When I finally threw a leg over a motorcycle and learned to ride, I discovered that I'd been right—riding a motorcycle is the closest a person can come to flying without actually leaving the ground.

The beauty of life—the camaraderie to be found among people who share the same passion for riding and being true—that's what motorcycle riding has shown me, and that's what I'd like to share with you. Whether you ride or not, whether you have your own motorcycle or not, listen up: that nomadic wanderlust is a beautiful part of all of us. It makes us the leaders of our own journeys in life. *VaVaVaVroom!*

Over the years since the publication of my previous book—*Bikerlady: Living & Riding Free*—and with the help of the half-dozen television shows in which I've appeared, I've had the great blessing to receive thousands of letters from men, women, and kids telling me about how my road philosophies, life history, and appearances have changed their lives. Little scooter-trash me changed lives? My little life inspired folks the world over? That's what I would deem living a life of purpose! To have inspired all these wonderful people has blessed me with utter humility and happy servitude. I write this book in honor of and for *you*.

Are you ready to face reality? Ride that road that awaits you? You should be, because that road is yours. It belongs to you, no one else, so, no excuses. Don't want to hear 'em. Been there, and it's a waste of breath. Don't tell me that you don't have what it takes to make this trip. Yeah, this trip called life. You've got all the resources.

See, this little biker chick is going to tell you to *stop* right where you are and *shut up* and *ride!* And I say that in the most caring way because I care about you enjoying a more fulfilling life. I want you to *roarrr* through life, whether you like to live out loud or be the strong, silent type.

Okay. Now that this Chrome Cowgirl has got your attention, listen to me carefully and answer these questions honestly:

The Wind Is Calling You

Wake up with a bunch of have to do's

But the wind is calling you . . .

the wind is calling you

Hold on tight,

life's a struggle and a fight

But the wind is calling you . . .

the wind is calling you . . .

Sasha © 2004 Road Diva Music

* If you could *fuel* your own dreams, what would you *do?*
* If you could *sit* in the saddle of your personality, who would you *be?*
* If you could *change* your life direction, what would you *change?*

And if you feel like mindlessly wandering the earth for a while, well that's just fine, too; there's no better way to do it than easy riding.

Here you are on your journey in life, your personal drama, your theater stage front and center. You're playing many different roles. Now I've got you where I want you. That contemplative expression . . . you're thinking . . . because you're at the crossroads now.

Welcome home, pioneer. You've come to the right landscape: the desert, sacred and sparse. Because now you've just deserted life as you know it. Take that chance to abandon all you know and let time take on a different dimension.

Let all your senses come alive, maximum overdrive. You know you want to!

Do you want to breathe deep and feel like your breath is infinitely expansive and wide? Do you want to be intoxicated by your sense of smell? Do you want to see with an awareness and depth that's supernatural? Do you want to feel as if your nerves can reach somewhere beyond the stars? Do you want to hear with crystal sonic quality? Do you want to feel like your whole soul just opened up?

Saddle up, girl! It's time to get roadacious on two wheels. It's time to expose yourself to the elements and roar to life spiritually, emotionally, and mentally, on your own motorcycle—your personal freedom machine. This vehicle is going to set you free.

Don't tell me you don't know how to ride or that you love to ride but don't have time. That's like saying you don't know how to breathe or you don't have time to breathe. It's in your nature. It's in your blood. It's in your smile. We were all born to ride. We were all born to be wild. There's no time for fear. It's two wheels all the way, now—no more crawling in a four-wheeled cage with that false sense of metal security walling you in and with your GPS telling you where you need to go. No. There's really no map. You have to discover the way, along the way.

You're standing tall on your own two mighty wheels, ready to take on the great adventure that will be the ride of your life. Creature comforts will now take on a different meaning. It's time to map the road that belongs to you and discover what awaits you. You've got the inner tools to do this: inspiration and intuition will be your map; insight and intellect will be the keys that ignite your own destiny. When journeying on two wheels, you'll use your inner tools to let loose that venerated character long hidden within you.

There is no more time left to waste, friends. Time has ticked by and will continue to tick by, leaving you behind in the dusty past dreaming about a future you can't see. Living and riding free means seizing your present moment. Summon your inner pioneer.

Fill 'er up, get your throttle ready, and kick-start the ride of your life. It's all about the here and the now—where anything is possible.

AS A RIDER, YOU KNOW THE WIND IS CALLING YOU TO SADDLE UP WHEN:

* The breeze that sweeps your face as you're walking toward your car feels like fingers draped in silk dancing across your skin. As you close yourself inside your car, you feel trapped. You are caged.
* Driving down the service road to get to the interstate entrance you can see the wind's power. Then a motorcycle pulls up next to you and you are seduced by the sound, its look, the unknown adventure that awaits it.
* While sitting at your desk you hear the familiar call of the wild, a distant rumble in your soul. You rise from your ergonomic prison to get a better view of the approaching animal.
* Exhaust pipes scream by in a flash of mirrored chrome. You feel your entire being reverberate with the sound, which tells you to claw your way out of routine and capture your dream to be set free upon that untamed steel beast.

Shut up and ride, pretty girl. The road waits for no one.

Sasha xo

"Sasha Belle"
The Chrome Cowgirl

P.S. When I say "shut up and ride," I mean it in the nicest way! Really I do!

"VaVaVaVroom" *Dennis Curnette*

Freedom is from within.

— *Frank Lloyd Wright, architect*

RIDELICIOUS
Tasty Freedom

Ridelicious: The ride is delicious freedom, a delicacy that explodes on the taste buds of your soul. Ridelicious is to scoot down the boulevard of dreams come true. Sink your teeth into something that gets your juices flowing and savor the mouthwatering experience of the open road, such as the sight of a fireball sunset, the scent of fresh sage dancing along a prairie's edge, the chilly temperature drop that happens while riding along a spectacular mountain pass. These are some of the flavorful ingredients of adventure. To taste freedom, to take a sip of unpredictable—this is ridelicious. And we all hunger for that taste of freedom. Motorcycles satisfy the craving.

Deliriously happy on my chrome horse, enjoying the ridelicious ride of life. Badlands, South Dakota. *Michael Lichter*

CHROME COWGIRL UP!

Chrome Cowgirls mirror the personality of the original cowgirls of the west. Here are some common characteristics about cowgirl attitude based upon the words found on the hallowed walls of the Cowgirl Hall of Fame in Texas, according to Ellen Reid Smith, author of *Cowgirl Smarts:*

- ★ Adventurous
- ★ Bold
- ★ Clever
- ★ Confident
- ★ Dedicated
- ★ Independent
- ★ Original
- ★ Passionate
- ★ Resourceful
- ★ Respected

- ★ Determined/Dauntless
- ★ Fearless
- ★ Genuine/Authentic
- ★ Hardworking
- ★ Honored
- ★ Steadfast/Loyal
- ★ Sense of Humor
- ★ Tough
- ★ True
- ★ Visionary

Like the original cowgirls of the Wild West, the early Chrome Cowgirls contributed to social reform by reshaping society's

Talk about a Legacy of Chrome Cowgirls!

In 1913, motorcycle riding became a family tradition. My mother, Diana, began riding in 1961. Her father and mother rode, as did both her grandparents. After Diana became a motorcyclist, her two sisters joined the family club. The summer of my 16th birthday, Mom bought me my first street legal bike. My now five-year-old daughter, Amber, is hooked on riding, so now we're five generations of motorcyclists! Mother and I would often take mother-daughter road trips. Almost every time people saw us someone would come up and say, "Wow, it's so cool to see women who ride. I've always loved bikes and would love to learn." Mother would gently reply, "Stop waiting to learn. Do it now and stop cheating yourself. You're going to LOVE it, and you'll be great at it!"

—Christine Marafioti-Firehock, motorcycle riding instructor and founder of Christine's KickSTART Motorcycle Training Series. She is a highly cool, pretty blond Chrome Cowgirl who is tough, sassy, and classy—a foxy rider indeed.

The road is my home.

"Cowgirl is an attitude, really. A pioneer spirit, a special American brand of courage. The Cowgirl faces life head on, lives by her own lights, makes no excuses. Cowgirls take stands, they speak up, they defend the things they hold dear."

— *Dale Evans*

Let me tell you what I think of bicycling. I think it has done more to emancipate women than anything else in the world. It gives women a feeling of freedom and self-reliance. I stand and rejoice every time I see a woman ride by on a wheel . . . the picture of free, untrammeled womanhood.

— *Susan B. Anthony, women's rights activist, in a* New York World *interview, February 2, 1896*

"Two wheels set me free long ago." The author on her yard-sale freedom machine.

expectations about how a woman should dress and what were acceptable activities in which she could engage. Prior to the emergence of the cowgirl, it wasn't acceptable for women to ride a horse or blaze trails solo. Same for the early female who loved riding two-wheeled freedom machines—she raised commotion for desiring to venture out on her own and take the road less traveled. Therefore, she had to be original, tough, and visionary to travel beyond the boundaries of society. She had to have confidence in her femininity and allow her unconventional girl power to shine through and strengthen her character. She had to hold her reigns tight and power through.

A Chrome Cowgirl is cowgirl-up tough: she doesn't back down and gives it all she's got, she toughens up and gets back on the horse when she's dusted, she never gives up, and she'll create a winning hand out of losing cards.

DITCH LIFE AS YOU KNOW IT

The quote from Susan B. Anthony pertains to the motorcycle, too. Motorcycles are a motorized version of the bicycle that set divine feminine energy free! Once you shut up and stop muttering excuses about how you can't do this or that, you discover that seemingly elusive path called your purpose. For many beautiful, talented, amazing, and loving folks, life is dull. Routine. Mundane. Sad and anxious. It is mediocre. These people have lost themselves. I know, I've been there! They don't have a map to help find themselves, and they can't MapQuest themselves a direction for their lives. They've totally strayed off the highway of life and are in a ditch. Their tired tires blew out because they couldn't take the same old ruts and potholes.

If you've found yourself stuck in life's ditch, don't worry; it's all excellent. Your radiator's spewing steam? That's your inner temperature regulator. You've thrown a rod, so it's time to get out of that cage in which you've been driving through life, that four-wheeled steel-and-glass prison that kept you falsely protected against the elements, and strike out on your new path, one that leads somewhere besides life's ditch. A "cage" in biker talk means a steel-and-glass–enclosed vehicle, but it seems to me that we live our lives in all kinds of cages, most of them less obvious than our cars. Part of

A Menu of 27 Chrome Cowgirl Characteristics

1. Is courageous and lives by her own set of rules.

2. Treats other Chrome Cowgirls ace-high and is quick to lend a helping hand.

3. Rides away from convention to lasso her dreams.

4. Is tough but soft and flaunts her power and femininity.

5. Is able to wrestle bullshit to the ground.

6. Pioneers new ways of thinking and doing things.

7. Can make home on the range on any road.

8. Rides for the brand and her riding buddies and is loyal to those with whom she rides; she watches the backs of her windsisters and brothers.

9. Enjoys advice but never lets anybody else decide what she can and can't do.

10. Welcomes new and exciting adventures.

11. Is great at rounding up a good time.

12. Wanders the vast terrain and lets her spirit loose to soar with the eagles.

13. Blazes new trails and travels beyond the homestead to discover golden opportunities.

14. Has a heart the size of Texas.

15. Will never sell her soul for a larger head stock.

16. Never lets another person, place, or thing break her spirit or stride.

17. Rides through fear and keeps her eye on the horizon.

18. Will, by hook or by crook, ride to the ends of the earth if she believes in something.

19. Keeps her Chrome Stallion or Chrome Mare in apple pie order and ceremonially names her horse.

20. Is keen on learning every aspect of riding well and expanding her territory.

21. Is a survivor and can instinctively figure out the lay of the land.

22. Is even-tempered at rude motorists and doesn't waste energy road raging.

23. Is quick to acknowledge the corn; honesty is her policy and her word is her bond.

24. Never passes another rider without waving "howdy do."

25. Is not a quitter, and therefore avoids complaining and complainers.

26. Is modest and avoids "gurgle and guts" braggart talk; instead, she praises her sister Chrome Cowgirls and brother Chrome Cowboys.

27. Honors Mother Nature and reveres Father Sky.

being a Chrome Cowgirl is discovering all the different cages in which we imprison ourselves.

And part of being a Chrome Cowgirl is escaping from those cages. It's time to ditch that vehicle that's got you caged in. That old way of thinking and doing, it's getting you nowhere. That vehicle isn't what's going to get you where you need to be. You need to ditch that life as you know it. Ditch what ain't working for you. Lots and lots of books out there teach you the mechanics of learning to ride and anything and everything you want to learn about all styles of riding. This little book is about the soul of riding, about prowling those open roads and *roarrring* down those highways Wild West style!

A "cage" in biker talk means an enclosed vehicle that encases its rider in glass and steel. *Road-inspired art by Sasha*

Time to taste some ridelicious freedom. Discover what's behind that burning desire to abandon life as you know it and take to the open road. That doesn't mean you can abandon responsibility. It means you get out there and live life to the fullest and embrace opportunity with your arms wide open in a rider's

Some Legendary Chrome Cowgirls!

Fran Crane — DISTANCE

Guinness Book of World Records record holder and Iron Butt Rally legend, the late Fran Crane loved to go the distance and push beyond the comfort zone to the land of dreams realized. Motorcycling, to her, was a testimony of one's dedication to personal achievement. Looking like an iron Godiva clad in her Aerostich riding suit, with her long hair flowing in the wind, she rode tall in that saddle, galloping 11,000 miles in eleven days in the Iron Butt Rally or sweeping across the country in a record 42 hours on her BMW. She enjoyed proving to people that she could do what they thought she could not do.

Della Crewe — STAMINA

Wherever Della went in the early 1900s, Trouble followed her. That is to say that Della and her trusty canine companion, Trouble, rode as a dynamic duo: she astride the motorcycle, he in the sidecar. Many people trailer their bikes to sunny destinations these days, but Della would forge onward through snow! Nothing would stop her. Obstacles made her chuckle. Della exemplified the cliché that when the going gets tough, the tough get going.

Bessie Stringfield — FAITH

After hearing the roar of an Indian motorcycle come to life, petite Bessie Stringfield prayed to Jesus to teach her to ride. She was sixteen, and it was the roaring twenties. The next day she saddled up, and away she went. Bessie lived and rode by the ways of Christ. Because of her lovely dark skin color, mean people would treat her something awful—though Bessie would remain steadfast and strong in her faith. She showed 'em all that she was a Queen of the Road by flipping a penny upon a map, whispering a prayer to the man upstairs, and riding off on her next journey.

Clara Wagner — COMPETITION

Clara Wagner achieved a perfect score in a 1910 FAM (Federation of American Motorcyclists) endurance competition, riding from Chicago to Indianapolis on a four-horsepower Wagner motorcycle built by her daddy, but she would be denied a trophy because she was a girl on a motorcycle. But the boys were so impressed with her competitive skills that they took up a collection and awarded her a gold pendant. She will forever be a winner to us starry-eyed female motorcyclists who ride to live.

Theresa Wallach — EXPLORATION

For Theresa, the planet was one big, giant, spinning globe to ride around. Her entire life revolved around everything having to do with motorcycles and The Rugged Road. She lived, breathed, worked, and shared the magic of all things motorcycles. Her explorations carried her around the globe on two wheels, beginning sometime in the 1920s. For Theresa, the uncharted roads made for better trailblazing!

embrace as you guide your motorcycle toward the ever-changing horizon. Twist the throttle, and desire roars to life. Discover your purpose, your God-given purpose. The wind will carry you anywhere you want to go. All you need to do is saddle up on your two wheels and ride.

Dot Robinson — LEADERSHIP

Along with Linda Dugeau, the ever-coiffed Dot Robinson led the Motor Maids, the first North American women's motorcycle club that today is the mother of all female clubs. With a lipstick case on her touring bike, she was dedicated to promoting a positive image for female motorcyclists, which remains the foundation of the club. Dot opened the door to many opportunities for women motorcyclists today. From leading a club, to racing a bike, to serving her community, to running a dealership, Dot was an example of stellar leadership and in today's world would make an excellent first female president for our beloved United States. Let's get a biker chick in office.

Adeline and Augusta Van Buren — UNCONVENTIONAL

They didn't have the right to vote, but they had the right to ride. Adeline and Augusta abandoned their socialite lives for lives as easy riders back in 1916. Back in those days, smooth pavement was as rare as a slime-free politician; it was muddy roads, meadows, gravel, and desert sand that tested the taste for adventure in these courageous gals. They made today's cross-country jaunt on a modern motorcycle look like a limo ride compared to their Wild West excursion. They wore pants, taboo for women in their time, and probably enjoyed many campfire chuckles at the stir they caused. In an unfettered cross-country journey, two sisters rode over convention and reinforced social and dress reform, all because they threw a leg over an Indian motorcycle and roared off for the adventure of a lifetime.

Diane Marafioti — EDUCATION

Diane was the definition of motorcycle mama. She wanted to mother the inner youngster in everyone and teach us all how to ride a motorcycle. She knew that a rider's education made the motorcycling experience the greatest high; hence, she cofounded the American Driving School. Diane also "mothered" the Lost Wheels Motorcycle Club, ran a school for riding, and drove an eighteen-wheeler. Her daughter Christine carries on her legacy with KickSTART. Christine sweetly remembers her mom saddling up all the kids on her motorcycle and going grocery shopping. Diane set out to teach the world how to live and ride free.

Vivian Bales — ADVENTURE

Vivian traveled by horse in her youth, but when teaching dance lessons gave her considerable pocket money, she sprung for a chrome horse that would unlock the greatest adventure of her life. In 1926, she purchased a Model B Harley-Davidson single, and "adventure tingled in my blood," she said. Vivian was loyal to her ever-loving friend, her Harley-Davidson motorcycle upon which she, in all her loveliness, would set out for high-time adventures around the country. Her enthusiasm for riding helped her become the first cover girl for Harley-Davidson's *Enthusiast* magazine.

Betty Robinson Fauls is the daughter of Dot Robinson, who was the first president of the Motor Maids all-female motorcycle club.

GETTING THE MOST OUT OF THE MOTORCYCLE LIFE

Freedom tastes good. Freedom on a motorcycle is ridelicious, my friends. It is a wind meditation. Those of us who love to ride become Zen masters in the art of wind meditation. The wind is where we can figure stuff out, let things go. All the fun reasons why people ride match up with all the finer points of life. A riding life is a life well spent and joyously experienced.

The motorcycle life teaches lessons that can help translate those wind meditations into your non-riding life, help you make every moment ridelicious.

I Feel Like I Can Be Myself When I Ride

All week long we delay the experience of being our true selves because of the many roles that we must fulfill. We delay the full experience of living except when we are on that motorcycle. In truth, who we are on that motorcycle is someone empowered, aware, vulnerable, and peaceful—we are still that same person in the office, at home, with our family or friends, even if those environments do not allow us to feel the same way we do on our motorcycles.

In reality, we are the same people when we're off our motorcycles as we are on them. If we don't feel as if we're allowed to be ourselves off our bikes, it's because we don't allow ourselves to be ourselves when we put the kickstand down and dismount. If you feel this way, give yourself permission to be the same person in the office, in your home, or at the supermarket as you are when you're flying down a twisting canyon road aboard your motorcycle. Deep down we are empowered, aware people. Remember, life is short, so live your dream. Be yourself, true.

Nicky Hero, 1955, Pensacola, Florida, is an AMA award-winning heroine to women in motorcycling. *Buddy Ford*

Throttle Rockin' Ridelicious
Definition of "Time" — the New Body Clock

Time relative to a clock is a relationship with moment. Time relative to events is a linear expression of where we've been and where we're going. The Ridelicious clock measures your movement around the sun. To cycle around the sun is a glorious mind refresher when all else seems to fail. Did you know that most philosophers agree that time does exist? They just don't know what it is! So, to say time waits for no one purely means that a clock won't stop ticking for anyone. But in the Ridelicious sense, time is moment. And there are only so many moments in a cycle around the sun, so it's really important to realize that every time you breathe, that's a moment. So, here's the equation:

Ridelicious Time = moments = breath = how many moments you've cycled around the sun.

The Ridelicious clock has nothing to do with age. It has to do with moments and breath. Age as a measure

of our existence on this earth simply doesn't exist if you love to ride. Only moments and breath count. It's like we were never born and we'll never die. Our souls are just occupying their individually precious space here on earth. So, we enjoy our existence without a sense of limitation. We enjoy our momentary existence, our momentary experiences. Moments count if they are truly lived in, truly acknowledged. Age defined as limitation is unfounded in the grand and immeasurable scope of Ridelicious time.

So, welcome that morning star we call the sun and be thankful that you've cycled around it for another time, easy-rider style. Each time you rock that throttle, it equals a breath. That's your new body clock, the Ridelicious clock. So, time waits for no one. And those racer chick girls know that, too!

It's Ridelicious time!

Riding Gives Me Peace of Mind

Motorcycle riding forces you to have peace of mind. It is the opportunity to think things through in one's solitude. Solitude is a precious gift. Most of us do not get to experience solitude because there is too much noise and interruption in our lives; but on a motorcycle, only you and the wind exist . . . and the roar of your scooter.

To have a peaceful mind is to have a still mind, and the only way to ride is with a still mind because on a motorcycle there is only room for the moment. You have to ride with the sharp focus of a straight razor, conscious of every movement, every sound, every smell around you to survive in a world of unconscious cages that can run you down. You don't have the luxury of drinking a nonfat latte while you chat on your cell phone on a motorcycle because the consequences are grave if you focus on anything but the moment. Talk about clearing the clutter from your mind! When you ride, you are right there. All of you, mind and body. There is no room on a bike for distraction.

That same peace of mind that we experience while we ride, we can bring into our everyday lives. We can take our still minds with us when we park our motorcycles. You'll be amazed at how wonderful the simplest things can be when savored with a still mind. I've heard lots of riding folks tell me "motorcycling saved my life." It saved mine, too, because motorcycles helped me savor my life.

Riding a Motorcycle Is the Ultimate Freedom

Living by one's own rules, one's own idea of how it ought to be, is to be an individual, not a clone. That's what it's all about. The motorcycle gives us freedom because we can abandon life as we know it and discover new ideas and new communities and ride away from the boundaries of mediocrity. No great leader was mediocre.

But they were themselves, whatever that may be—they didn't live by other people's expectations, they expected greatness from within, and they questioned authority. There is freedom in understanding and being understood. You're also exposed to the journey, and you are free to discover just what's around the bend. It's all unpredictable . . . and no matter how much you've prepared, there are always freewheeling moments up ahead.

Biker Chicks Rock!

No matter what kind of motorcycle you ride, you look great and feel better. A bonus provided by riding a motorcycle is that the activity is a fantastic confidence builder. You feel like you can do anything on a bike; you feel invincible. Chrome Cowgirls kick butt! When you're down and out, remember—you rock because you ride. So roll!

Chrome Cowgirl Road Slang

catchin' wind: No, this doesn't mean standing downwind when someone farts. This is when you're out there riding.

Chrome Charming: A suitor who arrives on his chrome horse and carries you off into the horizon.

Chrome Cowboy: A male pioneering motorcycle enthusiast.

Chrome Cowgirl: A female pioneering motorcycle enthusiast, aka biker chick.

chrome horse, chrome stallion, chrome mare, chrome filly: References to your motorcycle.

chromaddict: A rider who must chrome everything. I am not one of those.

chromate: Your soulmate who rides motorcycles.

curvaceousness: Having the skill, attitude, and confidence to handle the twists and turns, both in life and on a motorcycle. When you have a curvaceous attitude, you can lean with the twists and turns; in other words, go with the flow.

exitsty: This is the ecstasy of exiting the interstate or freeway and exploring some back road magic and mayhem. You can also experience exitsty when you exit the fast lane of life to cruise the slow lane, stopping and smelling the roses once in a while.

family: Any riding brother or sister you can call upon for anything; one who watches your back, and for whom you do the same. That person is with you for the journey of life no matter what chapter you're experiencing.

fastastic: Describes how awesomely your bike handles speed.

fastionista: Girls who like to ride fashionably fast in fast fashion.

Girls' Ride Out: This is the same as a Girls' Night Out but on motorcycles. It's all about having fun, making free-spirited merriment, and celebrating the wild and crazy you with the girls.

groovesational: That perfect, harmonious moment when your inner song is groovin' to the tires bopbumping along to the road grooves; oh, that's groovesational!

group therapy: What you experience when you're riding pack wild with a bunch of windsisterly Chrome Cowgirls.

High Noon moment: When you have a showdown with yourself about anything that's needing attention. You can also have a showdown with others over any matter needing attention. Sort of like a come-to-Jesus, nail-down-the-truth moment.

highway hero: A hot-looking Chrome Cowboy who rides to the rescue and offers you a quart of oil when you're low—and/or provides any other type of roadside assistance.

HipNoTies: This happens when you realize that, riding your motorcycle, oh my stars, you are so hip! No ties! You're a free bird. Just you and the road.

knock out the baffles!: What you tell someone when they need to quit their bellyachin' and timid livin' and live out loud, not in fear.

learning curve: When your curves hug the winding road's twists and turns as you learn that you are one bad-ass riding chick on the highway of life.

life behind bars: It's about accepting a free-spirited, happy life behind the handlebars of a motorcycle (without parole).

merry-go-round: When you attend a track day to learn to race, you go for a merry-go-round on the track.

motocure: The act of glamorizing, maintaining, and primping your motorcycle. Also a psyche term for curing non-motion sickness, as in "I need a motocure," which means you need to ride as a matter of life or death.

motorcycle mademoiselle: A riding chick who is all about the finer aspects of motorcycle riding and experiencing the elegant life at the same time.

motorcyclust: A rider with an insatiable appetite for all things motorcycle.

motorvational: Anything that inspires you to ride.

off to see the wizard: Taking off to have a dialogue with God on your motorcycle.

peace meal: A meal you purchase for a new windbrother or sister as a way of inviting a peaceful new friendship.

rev on: Do you got your rev on? In other words, are you head-to-toe in motion and looking fine on your ride?

ridelicious: Tasty motorcycle freedom.

riderotica: The orgasmic feeling you get in your heart, mind, and soul from riding a motorcycle and experiencing the exquisite adventure of it all.

riding soulo: Riding one with the Holy Spirit.

roadacious: Bold, brave, and courageous. Having a desire to chase every horizon.

roamance: What happens when you fall in love with the open road. Often used to describe a road romance, too, like falling in love with a Chrome Charming.

roll model: Any amazing female motorcycle rider who inspires you to roll on. It can even be you!

windsister: A female riding friend who becomes a lifelong sister through blood, i.e., motor oil runs through your veins!

wing-in-it: What you ask an angel for guidance anytime you need it on your journey, like when you're on your last tank of gas and funds are low, you'll say, "I'm just wing-in-it."

Sturgis bound!

Getting ready is the secret to success.

— Henry Ford, inventor and automaker

Route 2
THE ROAD TO RIDELICIOUS

The ride to Sturgis is my favorite of all rally journeys. It's my chance to fully become the Chrome Cowgirl that I am. That pioneering instinct bubbles to the surface, and I can charge a new path, explore, command my own destiny, and sit high in the saddle. I'm not on the fanciest bike, either. No, I'm not on the most comfortable touring motorcycle—but she's mine, and she's a part of my soul, and we go the distance together no matter what. On my motorcycle is where I can best let go and free my soul.

I begin to let go when it's time for that journey. I can hardly sleep. Butterflies fill me up because I'm so excited about the dawn of the new next day. I pack a million things I don't need and then totally unpack. I do this about five times. I've gotten good at it now. Before that, I'd bring way more than I'd ever wear. If I was gone for 20 days, well, that's 18 outfits. Now, if I'm gone 20 days . . . I bring five outfits with lots of room to get kitschy items and stop for random yard sales. The day before the journey it's like my brain begins to wind down a little bit . . . the sense of adventure really kicks in, and the adrenaline races through me in anticipation of that launch into the unknown on my scooter.

So, I saddle up on my chrome filly, pack her up with the essentials that include my tent and self-inflating sleeping mat, and *vavavavroom* I'm gone. I just like to get into the mindset of not expecting anything from my journey. Just get out there and immerse myself, come what may. Oh, I'm prepared for the journey, the best I can be . . . but I just want to let it unfold, lose control over the outcome. Let it be. That's a hard thing to do. But that's the key to joyriding through life. We have to silence what we think we know, and we have to just freakin' ride, man, ride.

Road Diary:

I can't believe that I can pack this much on my bike. How insane am I? I use about 12 bungees. There' are many easier ways to travel, like with the fancy tour packs and all. However, being the starving artist that I am, I like to be resourceful and just use what I've got. Hours at my temp job made it possible to afford this escape. I had to juggle the bill-paying thing . . . even though I don't have that many bills, I try and get those pipers paid. Whew.

I made really good time today. It was a hot one, too. Left Nashville early in the morning and got to this KOA campground just outside of Kansas City while it was still light. The tent is awesome. I set it up in record time. It was a quick-setup tent that I found in the trunk of an abandoned car from Alabama parked in the driveway of a rental I had in Nashville. Patrick, my beau, had to show me how to set it up. I felt dumb as a tack. The easiest thing in the world and I had a question mark dangling over my head. My beau just said in his southern drawl, "Well, honey, you just ain't holdin' your mouth right"—alluding to the silly face I made while trying to make it work. And there that blue and orange tent sits now with my bike Tigerlily gleefully poised beside it.

I think my Airhawk seat cover is slowly deflating . . . Ow! Or it wasn't inflated quite right because my ass hurts like hell. You see I have this seat on Tigerlily, beneath the Airhawk strap on-top thing, and it's a great seat, but it's not designed for the long haul . . . not this particular model seat. I did have a wide seat, which was better, oh sure it was, but, the problem was, the guys said that that seat made my butt look fat! I want my butt to look fast not fat! So off it came and on went the sleek profile one that hugged the frame and my butt. That damn seat looks hot, but my butt feels like I fell out of a truck and landed on the asphalt—ass fault first. Come to think of it, maybe my friend gave me this Airhawk he wasn't using anymore because it has a hole in it? I'll have to soak it in some soapy water to find out.

Anyway, tonight's meal consists of me going to Wal-Mart and getting some fruit, water, and eating my organic superfood bar. I don't like to be weighed down when I ride. I like to feel high . . . with high octane food fuel. I put super premium excellent gas in my motorcycle, and I want to feed myself the same way so that we can both be "on" at all times. I want this journey to shake me up. I need change, a new attitude. Oh, it was a hot ride today . . . swampy. I forgot to put sunblock on until it was too late so now I've got coon eyes and a Rudolph nose. The remedy? Just put blush or bronzer under your eyes to match the wind burn and sun burn. See, I went against my routine today which is tons of moisturizer, which I did do, and then top that with a healthy layer of 45 block, which I did not do. Later that afternoon, I did pick up some cheap 15 block at a dollar store and it sucked. So I got Neutrogena 70 block and that is no joke. You can bake out there and not see a line on you.

Off the beaten path, I discovered an abandoned farm town with streets under construction. That was weird. I guess they're planning on rebuilding the town. That would be nice . . . oh America the beautiful . . . what's happening to your little communities? Well there was a lone gas station on the edge of town where I loaded up with Propel water. Oh, I almost ran out of gas today. Ethanol reduces the distance I can go on a tank of gas. . . . I forgot to take that into consideration. Plus I was completely lost in the moment of the ride until Tigerlily coughed to let me know her tiny tank was near parched. I literally rolled into the station on fumes, smiling. All good.

EASY RIDE THROUGH LIFE, TWO-WHEEL STYLE

"Life ain't easy, Sasha," you may be saying. "I'm afraid to ride." Well, what's your definition of easy? Maybe you just need to change your perspective on that word.

Let's look at "easy," in concert with Merriam-Webster's dictionary:

eas·y [ee-zee]
1. *Not hard or difficult; requiring no great labor or effort.*

When you're an easy rider there's no great labor or effort involved. You want to become so good at riding that it requires no great effort. It will become second nature. But riding is a test of character. All that you truly are comes with ease, no matter how difficult any task involved may be. Riding is not hard or difficult. It is challenging in certain conditions. But riding becomes a part of you in a way that strengthens your mind, your body, and your very soul so that you can effortlessly and with abundant energy, easily take on that unpredictable path where your dream awaits you.

Every motorcycle journey offers a new beginning in life.
Road-inspired art, by Sasha

All difficult things have their origin in that which is easy, and great things in that which is small.

— *Lao Tzu, Chinese philosopher*

Once you've become one with your machine, you'll find the lack of everyday stress makes living very easy. Away from the complexity of routine in life, there is a place where the soul thrives in the moment of adventure. And then the way you look at life and engage life becomes easy, rebred, freespirited.

2. Free from pain, discomfort, worry, or care.

Out there on the open road, riding that motorcycle is one of the most pain-free experiences you can have because all of your pain, worry, bullshit gets blasted out in the wind. It doesn't exist. It's all about "Who cares?" and "What does it all matter anyway?" When you're out there riding, it's about you and that open road. There's no room on a bike for all that other stuff. Riding offers freedom from pain, discomfort, and worry in life.

3. Providing or conducive to ease or comfort; comfortable.

A motorcycle is an extension of your soul. So, it provides you with great comfort. It is like hot chocolate, a cold beer, a full-bodied glass of vino. Think about the thing that is your comfort food, so easy and gentle to the soul. That's what riding provides: ease and comfort. It is soothing.

4. Fond of or given to ease; easygoing; an easy disposition.

A dream relationship is one where you go with the flow. That easygoing style. Easy does it. Indeed, riding a motorcycle is easygoing at its best. Though not all bikes have an easy disposition, riding will put YOU in an easy disposition. You will just roll where the adventure leads you, easily rolling with the flow.

TRIP TIP
No matter if you're an expert or beginning motorcycle rider, read the highly entertaining *Complete Idiot's Guide to Motorcycles,* which will give you a really fun overview about this easy-ridin' and free-spirited sport.

5. *Not harsh or strict; lenient.*

There's nothing harsh about actually riding. The journey can be harsh, of course, but experience and preparation can ease the harshness of the elements. There's nothing strict about riding except you'd better strictly watch your ass out there and realize riding is life or death. Much like life is the choice of living or dying. The leniency of riding is, well, you get to be exactly who you want to be. You don't have to harshly adhere to corporate dress policy, adhere to strict workaholic deadlines and other people's demands on you. The ride lets you get lean on those things.

6. *Not burdensome or oppressive.*

There's nothing burdensome or oppressive about riding. Easy riding on two wheels is about lightening the load. See, you can't carry all your baggage on a motorcycle 'cause there's no room. The motorcycle is not oppressive. It keeps you from nothing. It'll carry you into the far reaches of the universe, if that's where your easy-riding butt is looking to haul itself.

7. *Not difficult to influence or overcome; compliant.*

Rest stop assured you will not need to be persuaded to seek freedom. It just burns in our yearning souls. It's part of our easy nomadic nature as human beasts. You'll want to be compliant to your nature . . . calling you into the easy wilds of the open road.

8. *Free from formality, constraint, or embarrassment.*

The only formality you'll be involved with here comes from your own road rituals. I light sage and mark the tires, sanctify the bike, flick ashes on the engine . . . that's my formality before I get my wiggle on and ride off. When it comes to have-to-do's or have-to-be's—ain't no formality. You can't wear seatbelts while you ride, so you're not constrained. The only constraint you'll come to know while riding is something quite imprisoning. It's called "fish" in cowgirl talk, or rain gear. No matter what, you can't make a fish look as pretty as a kitty. Toss any idea about embarrassment out the window when you ride wearing fish gear (unless you've got toilet paper hanging out

your butt when you leave the gas station bathroom, and you're acting all cool while you strut your stuff over to your chopper). Even if you drop your bike, that's not embarrassing because if you call on your feline nature, you can always offer up an attitude of, "I meant to do that," and gracefully pick it up.

9. *Effortlessly clear and fluent.*

Dig this: All things will become effortlessly clear and fluent the more time you spend cruising the open road. Your mind will be clear, and all the muck and mire that you spent years muddling through in thought will have been blasted out of your brain and left as road debris somewhere. You will begin to slow down and speak clearly. You won't have that insane rapid-fire dialogue that you're so used to in your ditched life. Oh, you'll end up speaking fluent road dialect, such as "let's throttle down and find a thrill." You will just go with the flow and become fluent with the experience of riding through life.

10. *Readily comprehended or mastered.*

The art of riding is an easy lifestyle to comprehend and can be easily mastered. There are no excuses and there's no time to waste. It's time to saddle up and peel out. Master the ride. Take lessons, expanding your knowledge, expand your horizons! Get on that open road, that beautiful wide-open highway with the great side trips to more great experiences. Discover kept secrets. Let go of all that bullshit. That's right—leave it in the ditch. Now you've mastered the ability to say, "'No. I'm not going to ride your path; I'm going to ride my path, the one God granted me. It's called the boulevard of my purpose."

11. *Not tight or constricting: an easy fit.*

There's plenty of elbow room on a motorcycle. Lots of air to breathe, too. You want to be cradled in your seat, comfortably reaching the controls of the bike. A ride that fits you snug pretty much means you're going to spend a lot more time in the saddle. It'll be easy to ride all those miles and not stop all the time. You won't want to stop. Set up your motorcycle so it is an easy fit, a love affair.

12. *Not forced or hurried; moderate; an easy pace.*

Even if you're clocking 75-plus miles per hour, gunning that throttle wide open, friends, you're still at an easy pace. There's nothing frantic happening. You're not forced to do anything except stop for gas and, well, you do have to recognize the speed limit, so you may have to slow. You'll feel your whole life growing much more moderate once you embark upon the adventure to become an easy-riding fool for the open road.

13. *Not steep; gradual.*

You know those metaphorical mountains we must climb in life when trying to reach our goals? With the bike, you've got a nice, easy grade to tackle; the rise to the top is gradual, not fearful and steep so you lose sight of your goal. We're talking a steady and gradual cruising altitude here. That goal is in sight at all times, even when you don't know what's around the bend. Nice and easy. No fear. Only faith.

GETTING IN THE ZONE

The motorcycle selection process involves a highly personal choice, much like religion. Riding will be a form of religion for you now, so you need to choose the right motorcycle that will administer to your riding style. Choose a vehicle that will improve your great escape on two wheels.

Gettin' in the Zone, Baby

"I would not waste my life in friction when it could be turned into momentum."
— Frances Elizabeth Caroline Willard, suffragist, author, educator

That Friction Zone is your power play. Power is at the tip of your clutch and throttle fingers. Once you feel and become one with the energy of the Friction Zone in your clutch hand, you will twist that throttle grip and turn the gasoline in the carb into momentum. That moment of friction is the clutch engaging and transmitting the power of the engine to the rear wheel as you intuitively pour the right amount of gasoline by use of the throttle. It's like a recipe . . . dash of this, cup of that, and this fine act of friction and momentum is performed. The gentle massage of that clutch lever with your fingertips, used with the lovely roll of the throttle, releases the steel horse from the gate. Learning to finesse the Zone is like experiencing great sex. The control is intoxicating.

THE BIG WHAT-IF FIBS THAT HOLD YOU BACK

★ *What if I can't learn how to ride a motorcycle?* Dakota began riding a Harley at 13 years old, when she became a stunt rider for Hardly Angels motorcycle dance line. Can you ride a bicycle? Then you can learn to ride a motorcycle.

★ *What if I'm scared to ride a motorcycle?* Everybody is scared the first time they learn to ride. It's fear of the unknown. Lack of confidence. But, oh girl, once you get on the training course you're going to have so much fun that you'll ride right past that silly fear. Bye-bye, fear. Move past your comfort zone, and there's a huge adventure just waiting for you on two wheels.

★ *What if I can't pick up the bike if I drop it?* So what! That's all I've got to say. There are ways to pick it up, but you know, I'm not able to pick up lots of bikes, but that doesn't stop me from riding.

★ *What if I can't handle the size of a motorcycle?* Oh how we ponder size in everything we approach. Yes, size does matter, and you can handle it. Make it fit through customizing a few things or select a motorcycle that can fit you like a glove. Feel free to jet around on a scooter, too, in the beginning. They're loads of fun. My first bike was a spankin' new Harley-Davidson Sportster. Read my first book *Bikerlady: Living & Riding Free!* to find out how I got that pussy cat of a cycle.

★ *What if I don't know how to fix my own bike?* There are a lot of people who don't know the first thing about fixing their own motorcycles. Sure, it's great to know the basic mechanics and how things sort of work. But if that's not your bag, don't worry. Just find out the proper name for what you might call a thingy when you think you've narrowed down your bike's ailment.

★ *What if I can't afford to buy a motorcycle?* There are loads of inexpensive bikes out there for sale just waiting for your hot little dollars in exchange for your cool-looking butt in the saddle. Remember that Asia and Europe consider the motorcycle not as a luxury but as a viable and primary mode of transportation. In some locations, you may see a whole family crammed onto one bike!

Having the gift of artistic vision when designing a custom motorcycle is overwhelming. To be able to take raw materials with no shape and create a machine with individual identity can only be compared to the feeling I get when riding it for the first time . . . uninhibited.

— *Dawn Norakas, bike builder,*
Stinger Custom Cycles

★ *What will people think of me if I ride a motorcycle?* W.O.W. (With Out Words) is the first word folks will say, followed by a whistle and smile, both men and women. Children will applaud and do somersaults in the back seat of the car to get you to wave at them. Everywhere you go you kick up a good row just for being a Chrome Cowgirl roaming the open roads.

And then the best:
★ *What will my family or job think of me if I ride a motorcycle because then I'll have to carve time for me and not attend to all their needs all the time!* Honey, just set that laundry basket down, walk away from that office, tell the man to go do the grocery shopping. Riding a motorcycle is the ultimate *me* time. The moment your bike keys are in your hand, you've just stepped into the zone of me time.

The motorcycle is an extension of the Chrome Cowgirl. It's an offspring, birthed from you and the manufacturer. That motorcycle was destined to be yours. The right motorcycle that you acquire is like finding the right relationship. It's the perfect match. And then, once you're smitten with this very essential and organic activity of riding, you

This cool chopper was transformed by Seeger Cycle of North Ridgeville, Ohio, with Chrome Fusion's (Las Vegas, Nevada) tigerlily art on the tank and fenders.

can't imagine life without your divine motorcycle, your "horse" power. This is why riders choose to name their motorcycles. Nicknaming your chrome filly is a sweet way to bond with your motobeast.

CHOOSE YOUR SCOOT STYLE!

Before you decide on a style of motorcycle, you first need to ask yourself some questions about the style of riding you intend to do. And you may be interested in a combo of styles.

* ✶ *Cruisin':* Do you want to just scoot around town, go for a weekend jaunt? Show off the motorcycle? Do a few excursions but keep mostly to your home area?
* ✶ *Distance:* Do you intend to marry that saddle and live in it? Ride several hundred miles a day? Visit far and distant rallies and events?

Style is the perfection of a point of view.

— *Richard Eberhart, poet*

- ★ *Speed:* Do you like to crotch rocket? Zip around a track? Test your curvaceous nature in the tight twisties?
- ★ *Commuting:* Do you intend to commute to work, run a few errands? Are you looking for a convenient mode of transportation?
- ★ *Off-road:* Do you want to get dirty and go off road, explore the mountains, or motocross?

And what style of bike?

- ★ *Touring:* A touring bike is one that's set up to go the distance comfortably. Touring bikes can sometimes be a combination of sport-touring or cruiser-touring. These bikes have lots of modern conveniences for the wayward traveler, such as stereos, GPS units, storage compartments, CD players, and much more. These bikes tend to be heavier and taller than others but can be set up to fit the smaller skilled rider.

Get on your motorcycle and ride, ride, ride—then you will truly discover who you are; your soul and spirit are one. Your chopper is the foundation upon which you and it were built to travel through life and experience things regular people only dream about. Treat her well and treat yourself great, too. Then you will never be alone. You will always have your true companion with you and don't forget even she needs a day at the spa every now and then.

— Athena "Chickie" Ransom,
Vagabond Chopper Company

Dolled up in Icon leathers, this Chrome Cowgirl safely gallops along the road in style.
Michele Lanci-Altomare

★ *Cruiser:* A cruiser is great because it can be used for lots of different styles of riding. A cruiser can be easily customized because there are so many aftermarket companies that provide products for all types of cruisers. Harley-Davidson makes the most popular cruiser bike in the marketplace. Cruisers are great for kicked-back, beefy riding.

★ *Custom:* These types of bikes are mostly for show and short distances but can be set up for the long haul. Custom bike builders will create this bike, you can buy a kit bike and create your own, or you can just get all the parts and assemble it yourself, but you ought to get it checked out by a seasoned builder or mechanic before you ride it. These rides usually cost lots of money but look so cool. This is the couture version of riding.

★ *Sport/Super Sport:* If you want to tear up the track, tackle some back road twisties, have a sporty look, then this type of bike is for you. It's compact, and the riding position is more one of hovering over the controls rather than sitting straight in the saddle like a cruiser. This is for the Jane Bond in you.

**Before everything else,
getting ready is the secret to success.**

— *Henry Ford, inventor and automaker*

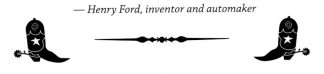

★ *Dual-Purpose:* You can ride on road or off road with a dual-purpose motorcycle. These bikes can make fun commuter bikes, too. Say you're cruising along a corn field and the blacktop runs out and you find yourself nearly motocrossing through the fields 'til you get to some more blacktop. This style is an excellent choice if you're into adventure riding. And if you're a globetrotter visiting places with purely unpredictable thoroughfares, or you simply enjoy touring the wild back roads, switching from asphalt to earth, this is a great type of bike.

★ *Off-road:* This is purely for the dirty girls, the girls who love to play in the dirt. Get muddy, get dusty. Wear Mother Earth like a fine mineral makeup. Get on your dirty bike and ride the whoopdeedo's, singing out "whoopdeedo!"

MAKE IT FIT

Sometimes there's a bike that is a close fit, like a fabulous pair of shoes, but we've got to do a little finagling to get that glove fit happening. Customizing one's motorcycle is an extension of one's soul, mind you, and is as much fun as nesting in a brand-new home. It is yours, and that bike reflects you in every way.

Here are some tips:

★ *controls:* You can adjust the handgrips to fit your hand positioning. If the clutch is too stiff, you can get an EZ clutch lever. If the grips are too large, you can get thinner-profile grips. If your feet feel stretched out too far, you can switch positioning of the foot pegs and controls. You can change out the type of footrests and controls, too.

★ *seat:* Get rid of that wide-load seat and find a narrow touring seat so that your legs don't feel like you're splayed on an OBGYN table. Also, there are thinner stuffed seats that hug the frame better, seats that scooch you up toward the tank more. The aftermarket provides all kinds of seats that allow you to reach the ground.

★ *shoes:* I'm a petite chick, so I wear the highest heeled boots I can find that are functional for riding. They also have thick heels to stabilize me when my feet are on the ground or for when I need to do some fancy maneuvering to get my bike through sand or another type of challenging riding surface. Stiletto heels don't provide enough of a contact patch with the ground to allow you to control your motorcycle, but they look sexy! Get oil-resistant soles glued on your kicks, too. I love shoes. Can you tell?

My helmet is like my cowgirl hat. *Michele Lanci-Altomare*

★ *mirrors:* Mirrors that provide good rearward vision help you survey the land behind you, so get the best pair you can afford. If you don't want gigantic Dumbo-eared mirrors, well, I love the tiny fashion mirrors, too.

★ *handlebars:* I'm an ape hangin' girl myself. I dig how they look and how functional they are for my short arms. Beach bars are a no-go for me because once I turn the handlebars I no longer have a handle on my bars. My hand is long gone from the grip. Those bars feel like they're down the block and I'm catching up with them. Buck horn bars . . . yucky for me. I feel like my wrists are locked in handcuffs all cramped up and locked in. Oh, I adore sport bars, too. Both sport handlebars and sport bars where the boys hang out.

There are loads of books and DVDs about customizing your bike, from painting it, to chroming it, to making it a faster pussycat. As the resourceful hippie gypsy biker chixie that I am, however, I encourage masterpiece arts and crafts magic, self-created by you, be applied to your ride. Here are some cheeky crafty custom ideas for fun.

CHEEKY CRAFT CUSTOM IDEAS

* ✭ Decorate your handlebars with Hula-Hoop identi-tape.
* ✭ Super glue crystals and stones onto your motorcycle.
* ✭ Embellish your oil tank, derby cover, license plate holder, or gas cap with all kinds of findings, jewels, medallions, and stickers.
* ✭ A helmet is like your cowgirl hat, and it is a blank canvas to express your personality in any mixed-media art form you'd like.
* ✭ Get crafty with reflective tape. Cut it into shapes and stick reflective patches on your jacket and motorcycle. Be seen!

Other Cheeky Crafty Things You Can Do with Discarded Motorcycle Pieces

* ✭ *Hang your old burned-out tire as a welcome wreath on your garage door.* Get crafty and put some pretty silk flowers on it and then get a piece of cardboard cut into a circle. Cover it with aluminum foil, and then stick on those black and chrome mailbox letters and spell out "Well, come on in!" and mount it inside the tire.

* ✭ *Make a clock out of a brake rotor plate.* Take a used rotor, clean it up. Mount an atomic clock timepiece to it.

* ✭ *Frame a canvas out of ape hanger handlebars.* Mount the handlebars to a wood strip. Mount the wood strip to the wood portion of the finished canvas. Hang on the wall with a heavyweight mount.

* ✭ *Build a gas tank flower pot.* Clean out the inside of a peanut tank. In the middle of it, cut out a long, narrow rectangle, and while you're at it, enlarge the drainage hole underneath. Clip and curve under the sharp edges. Keep the gas cap area intact! Decorate the tank as you wish. Fill about half an inch of the bottom with small stones, but keep the drain area as clear as possible. Fill with dirt. Place a hearty plant inside. You can plant flowers, too.

* ✭ *Create rearview mirror candle holders.* You can leave the glass on the mirrors. Just mount the rearview arms onto a strip of decorative wood. Turn the mirrors so they face the ceiling. Burn some wax, drip it on the mirror and then fasten a flat-bottomed candle on each of them.

* ✭ *Make a license-plate holder photo frame.* Get a sturdy piece of cardboard and create a frame out of it. Trim the top of the cardboard to about 1/8 inch shorter than the bottom. Cut out a piece of photo frame plastic to match the size of the license-plate frame. Lay it into the frame. Glue the cardboard to the inside edge of the license-plate holder, but don't seal the top part of the

- ★ Make your own tool bag or road beauty bag! Take an old small leather purse and modify it to fit on your sissy bar, on your handlebars, or as a fork bag to carry your road stuff.
- ★ Zip ties are great for mounting odd treasures onto your handlebars.

Be prepared to spend money on your sexy, cool motorcycle, all right girls? I've got plenty of dog-eared parts catalogs in my book bag that I tote around. Many times you'll find me cozy in a corner of some café salivating over motorclothes and related products in

cardboard, and be sure not to glue the plastic inside. Get some small circle Velcro. Put some Velcro receivers on the back of the cardboard license-plate frame you made. Put some Velcro holders on a photo stand and mount that to the back of the cardboard. Size your photo to the frame and slip it into the top of the frame.

- ★ *Build an engine block glass coffee table.* This is heavy. You need a big piece of wood to mount the engine on. You can use granite, too, but that's tricky. Then you need to create metal brackets to hold the engine onto the wood. I suggest getting crafty with your welding technique for this one. Place clear rubber mounting pieces on the top of the engine cases. On top of this you will put a piece of precut glass with sanded edges. If you want to get really fancy, get an etching kit and etch some fun scroll designs onto the glass top corners.

- ★ *Build fender side tables.* Take a fender and decorate it as you wish. Mount it onto a piece of decorative wood or stone by adhering metal fasteners inside the fender, then bolt it down onto the base. Place small clear rubber mounting pieces on top of the fender and place glass as mentioned above. You can also include custom-cut, narrow, straight drag pipes as support pieces on each edge.

- ★ *Create an engine cover hors d'oeuvre tray.* Clean an engine cover really well to the point of brand-new sparkle inside. Coat the inside with a food-safe powder coat. Load it with chips and salsa.

- ★ *Create wall art.* Get a big canvas and create a mixed-media piece of motorcycle journey art that is part decoupage of photos from your journey, part doodles you draw during the journey, part treasures you find along the road, and part smaller used motorcycle parts and hang it in your office, your den, your kitchen . . . any place you want to feel like you're still out there on the ride!

Even my oil bag's got personality.

a Drag Specialties, J&P, Custom Chrome, Tucker Rocky, Biker's Choice, or lots of other independent supply catalogs. Of course, a biker chick Chrome Cowgirl or a racy motorcycle babe also loves her motorcycle magazines. We devour those rags like a secret to the perfect diet . . . and riding is the secret to that perfect diet because it satisfies your cravings and completely fills your body, mind, and soul with appetizing savoir faire! Motorcycle riding is an appetite suppressant, and the only hunger you feel is a ravenous appetite for an open-road adventure.

MOTOR-CIRCLES

The *circle*, the *cycle*, spinning, and turning are powerful and lighthearted activities. There is a correlation between motor*cycles* and hooping *circles*—all very hip-swinging.

SIPDE AND T-CLOCS

Taking off for your ride without inspecting your motorcycle is sort of like walking out of a fancy restaurant restroom without checking to see if your skirt is tucked in or if there's lipstick smudged on your teeth, except that the consequences are far more severe. Disastrous. Inspecting your ride saves your life, plus it protects you from losing parts that might fly off your bike and hit random riders and drivers.

As the wheels turn in circles, so goes my Hula-Hoop. My hips guide the ride. Life cycles full circle on a motorcycle. *Michele Lanci-Altomare*

Hoops activate energy centers of the body and stimulate a sense of vitality, playfulness, and exhilaration. Hoops are like training wheels, stimulating my ability to gyrate with joyful, unabashed sensuality. The act of spinning and turning accelerates a primal quickening in my body. I feel sweaty, super-charged and alive! Every time I turn in the hoop, I return back to a place of self acceptance. The music pumps and I'm in the pocket, hooping to the funky grooves! I feel on-fire with inspiration and energy. I remember that my body is a holy temple and that no matter how it looks, it is good. I remember that hip-swinging is my birthright. And I remember that pleasure is good. For me, hoopdance is a way to cycle back to a sense of wholeness. Beginnings become endings which become beginnings again. Anything is possible. I am so grateful!

— *Christabel Zamor, CEO, HoopGirl Inc.,*
and a professional hoop dancer

The T-CLOCS Inspection

The T-CLOCS concept was developed by the Motorcycle Safety Foundation as a mnemonic device to help riders remember the routine items to inspect before riding a motorcycle. Use the T-CLOCS method to inspect your motorcycle before you ride or buy one, and use it as a brief maintenance guideline.

T-CLOCS—The Motorcycle
T—Tires & Wheels
C—Controls
L—Lights
O—Oil

C—Chassis
S—Kickstand and Centerstand

T-CLOCS—The Rider
T—Teeth—Check to see if anything is in your teeth.
C—Crown—Strap and adjust your helmet and hair.
L—Lips—Freshen the lipstick while adjusting mirrors.
O—On Stage—Your performance is life or death. Be seen. The chrome Pony Express stage is set.
C—Calm—Breathe deep and smile. Zen is your friend.
S—Spirit—Say a gratitude prayer.

TIRES AND WHEELS

Tires: Check pressure (cold), survey the tread condition; make sure there are no cuts, weird bulges, or odd things hanging out of the grooves. Note: check tire pressure often!;
Wheels: Spokes should be firmly hanging tough and rims nice and straight, no rim shimmies when you flex that rim;
Brakes: Nice and firm; good pad density, no leaky or kinky hoses or cables.

CONTROLS

Levers: Lubed and in a comfortable cruising position, nuts and bolts are tight;
Cables: Lubed, no kinks, no tears or fraying, no binding or stretching; make sure all cables are routed well;
Hoses: Check for leaks or wear and tear; make sure all are properly routed;
Throttle: Snappy response; no play; cables are secure in housing.

LIGHTS

Brakes, Turn Signals, and Taillights: All aglow and operating in sync with the controls;
Headlight: All aglow and aimed right, and make sure it's secure in the housing;
Lenses: Check for cracks and condensation; should be tight and clean;
Reflectors: Check that they are clean and secure and add more if needed;

Battery: Check that it is clean and dry; check fluid level and connectors; check for signs of damage, nothing kinked or loose; check vent tube;
Wiring: Check for pinching or fraying; security and routing.

OIL AND FLUIDS

Levels: Check brake fluid, oil, final drive, transmission, coolant, fuel;
Leaks: Check everywhere for leaks;
Condition: Check for freshness.

CHASSIS

Frame: Check excessive wear spots, look for cracks, or splits in the paint; manipulate the fork and check that it's secure, check fork seals, check your fork oil!;
Suspension: Check adjustment for load; look for wear, no leaks, smooth movement;
Fenders: Make sure those suckers are secure on there and that there's no rubbing against the tires;
Chain or belt: Check tension; lube; look for wear or kinks;
Fasteners: Check for loose nuts or bolts; batten down the fasteners!

STANDS

Sidestand: Retracts firmly; spring intact, holds position well;
Centerstand: Retracts firmly, not loose or flimsy, holds firm position.

Of course, before a rider takes to the saddle, there is a self-inspection, too. Inspect yourself! So you can sit high in the saddle.

The Motorcycle Safety Foundation's (MSF) instruction book for riding encourages the rider to check out the scene. Details! Details! Absorb every bit of visual information you possibly can. See what I mean: *Author's Note: For in-depth technical riding instructions, please refer to the motorcycle safety instruction books published by Motorbooks* (Ride Hard, Ride Smart *and* How to Ride a Motorcycle) *as well as those produced by the Motorcycle Safety Foundation. For more information, check out the reference section in the appendices.*

ESP: EXTRAORDINARY SELF-PROTECTION

As a Chrome Cowgirl, you will focus on your path and keep your distance from the saboteurs who would distract you from your destination. You are in full command of your destiny. This is why you must develop your alternative ESP (Extraordinary Self-Protection). Get dialed into all your senses. Remember, you are not ordinary; you are *extraordinary,* eons beyond ordinary. You ride and you're embarking upon adventures and wonderful, thrilling challenges! Therefore, you must protect your holy *self* to be whole in body, mind, and soul when you're out there cruising or racing down the roads or racetracks that compose the highway of life. *Protection* is in the form of prayer . . . ah, sweet prayer, setting boundaries, knowing your territory and talents, understanding how to always be positive no matter what. ESP = Confidence.

SIPDE AND SEE

In order to really sip some tasty, ridelicious motorcycle freedom, you need to protect your space. Ride your ground. The old MSF lesson was **Scan, Identify, Predict, Decide, Execute.** SIPDE. The new saying the MSF came up with is **Search, Evaluate, Execute.** SEE. Cool, it's all the same, but I like the old one; I'm a SIPDE girl:

The Chrome Cowgirl is the queen of awareness. She is fully exposed to the moment, and her every sense is alive. She can ride up on a scene and absorb every detail. She will view a situation with

"Inspect yourself! Hey Hey Hey Hey!"

"I.N.S.P.E.C.T., find out what it means to me!"
INSPECT YOURSELF before you saddle up!
The BEAUTY system was developed by the author. Because that radiant beauty in and out must be in check before any horsepower is produced!

BEAUTY
Make sure you've got on your facial lotions, sunblock, lip balm, and lipstick and that your hair is coolly styled for the ride. You are one hot mama.

ENSEMBLE
Are you totally femme fatale, dressed and ready for riding success? Do you have your nerdy rain gear packed and easily accessible? Are you zipped up and snapped down so nothing flaps? Electric gear plugged in?

ATTITUDE
Calm, cool, collected, and confident. It's all good, even when you feel a little blue, Never ride angry . . . it causes wrinkles and road rage. Riding is a happy event.

UNDERSTAND
Understand your route and your options if you encounter unexpected road snafus. Commit to memory your route in sections or write it with China marker on the bottom of your windshield or display the directions through the see-through clear pouch on your tank bag.

TIME
Not that we're living by the clock, but it's good to factor in time zone changes, if you care. Keep in mind rush hour traffic during your trip. Because you are not in a rush. Depart as early in the day as you can . . . it's so much fun to watch the sunrise.

YOU
YOU are precious. Safety at all times. This is your life, precious girl. Ah, the beauty of life. You are handmade, uniquely crafted at the hands of the creator. What do we do with handmade gifts? We treasure them. Let's treasure you. Ride strong and treasure-minded.

FOCUS! FOCUS! FOCUS!	Concentrate on your intended path of travel and move within traffic while maintaining adequate space in all directions.	Focus on your own path. Forget about everyone else. Keep your distance from people and circumstances that will distract you and sabotage your destination. Develop your ESP (Extraordinary Self-Protection).
AIM!	Aim your vision well ahead by keeping your eyes up.	Don't be downcast. Keep an eye on the prize that awaits you on the horizon ahead!
SURVEY!	Force your eyes to move frequently so that you will receive a wide field of information.	Details! Get into the mindset of hyperawareness. Don't let life pass you by and don't miss cool opportunities because you didn't notice them.

a new set of eyes every time. This kind of awareness is essential to protect herself when she rides. Riding ignites intuition and heightens anticipation like a never-ending state of expectation. The Chrome Cowgirl commands her position on the road like a queen.

Remember: Common sense while riding keeps you from chewin' gravel. Ride within your skill level and know that the wisest decisions are usually based on common smarts and calm, cool decision-making skills. The road is always going to teach you something new, so let it. You don't know everything. And I'll keep on stressing how important it is to get savvy on different riding styles and be excited about drinking from that foundation of knowledge anytime you can in any way you can. Bottom line? If you don't obey the basic codes of respecting your chrome stallion's mechanics, if you don't learn good riding techniques, the road will definitely knock some sense into you.

CHOOSE A ROUTE, LEAVE THE PAST BEHIND: HAVING THE COURAGE TO CHANGE

The truth about ourselves is found on the adventure, away from routine, away from manmade timelines and demands. Out there in the vast landscape lies new opportunity to be harvested. This is where we hear the spirit strongly suggest to us "go further, release fear" because going beyond the bounds of human confines is where we find our wild freedom. Thus the truth in our souls, the joy in our hearts, and the very cores of our being are revealed.

Life is either a daring adventure, or nothing.
To keep our faces toward change
and behave like free spirits in the presence of fate
is strength undefeatable.

— Helen Adams Keller,
excerpt from "Let Us Have Faith," 1940

FUEL FOR THOUGHT

"Ride your own ride," said the spectacular Fran Crane. Skert, another savvy long-distance Iron Butt rider, echoes the motto in her riding seminars. To ride your own ride is the key to experiencing radical joy on a motorcycle. It's your journey, your personality, your life, your vehicle, your choices, and your loyalty to yourself to ride within your own set of riding skills and abilities.

Music and motorcycles reflect my heart and soul. *Pat Lassiter*

Mapping your destiny is about the serious question: where do you want your life to end up? Life is brief. And the motorcycle life lives in the moment. The wonderful people who are in this community appear ageless because they are. When folks who are not familiar with the biker lifestyle stumble upon us, they always think, Grow up! They think this because we are like children on a playground. We not only talk about our goals and what we want to be, we go for it . . . even if it takes us a lifetime. We choose our own storylines in life. We have fantastic stories filled with all kinds of trauma, drama, and comedy. Our lives are documentary, reality—we embrace the gambit of emotions. We are works of art!

Queen of the Road is a chick in charge of her journey. She's totally aware of everything around her. Because of that, no one can run her down or get in her way. She's a good judge of road character. She's got great intuition and can predict what another driver might do; therefore, she owns the road accordingly. *Road inspired art by Sasha.*

THE ELEMENT OF SURPRISE

The motorcycle is the ideal vehicle to expose you to the elements . . . not only the Mother Earth natural elements, but the element of surprise! So sweet is the element of surprise upon the chosen route. Some of these pit stops along the way can be ugly, brilliant happenstances that curve you around an unexpected bend leading you to a turning point in life. If planned, these turning points may never have happened; it's in the beauty of an unplanned stop that the long-awaited spark happens.

Sparks fly and so do pigs, once you really get to understand what this motorcycle life is all about. You can manifest your dreams, and the fat lady will sing and hell will freeze over. Because anything is possible. Just choose your route. Or let a route choose you. Select a direction to travel. Embrace the horizon that you're zooming toward.

Sometimes I just want to wander the open highways. I just have a need for speed, and I want to race my motorcycle along the landscape and feel the wind just rush over me. Other times, I want to be quiet and meander along a small back road and not go over 50 miles per hour. I just want to be a drifter. The route can be a moody choice. A slow pace lets the wind caress your soul a bit more gently if you're feeling injured or confused. Maybe we just want to quietly commune with nature back there on a two-lane winding road.

Just recently, my route changed. I fought that change, too, friends. I've never been married . . . always been the gypsy rider,

Playing music is not much different than negotiating the road with a motorcycle. If you stay steady and slow and sure of what you're doing, the world will meet you, on your terms.

— *Lisa Lynne, Windham Hill Records,*
Celtic harpist and motorcyclist

riding solo on my long journeys. But then I met a Chrome Cowboy who encouraged me to live my dreams more than ever before. He was living his, this biker dude, this successful bass player, vintage guitar collector, and motorcycle enthusiast. This man was all about music and motorcycles.

Just like me.

He asked me to marry him, and I said yes, of course! Here was a highway to heaven for me, folks! And I was a bit reluctant. I've always been a free spirit, independent out here. Sure, I'd love a companion, especially a fellow who encourages my dreams and wants to provide me with a new way of living in order to achieve those dreams . . . marriage. Coupledom. Why, I had to saddle up on Tigerlily and take off on a 3,500-mile journey to think about this. It just didn't seem real. I had become a prisoner to routine . . . my own struggle and routine because I forgot that indeed I could choose another route! At any time! And perhaps I could have chosen another route to get to my dreams even without the encouragement of this dashing Chrome Charming. Though, truly, I had to understand the gift this great person was offering me, as a man who would be a very important part of my life story as my life partner.

I had to have the courage to change, to examine the role this man would have in my life and how my life would be different.

BAD ASS WITH PISTOL-PACKIN' CLASS

"Bad ass with class" is how my buddy, leather designer Jan Rousseaux, describes us female motorcycle riders. She has designed some outrageous riding clothing for me.

That's how I like to think of us Chrome Cowgirls: classy, sassy, and bad assy. Riding a motorcycle cleared up a lot of insecurities for me. All my life I had a confidence issue. Being a wallflower growing up, I didn't fit in, and I wasn't popular. I was picked as a, big sigh, last resort for all sports. Just a little hippy chick at heart. Immersing myself in music and books, I'd dream about the great escape—riding off somewhere cool. My motorcycle bolsters my confidence, inspires me to live my dreams and now this geek can fit in anywhere she goes! The motorcycle makes it okay for me to be me. Quirks, oddities, and

Fastionista. The strength is in being totally feminine, total girl power. Dig the Jan Rousseaux custom-designed leathers! Motorcycle built by J.C. at Chrome and Custom Cycles.
Karen Fuchs

ideologies. Most of all, like any of us, I just want to live my life my way, without apology. My pistol-packing attitude is to be a Chrome Cowgirl pioneering her own path, in harmony with her soul and a greater spirit. Doing the right thing and answering to no one. And just around the corner, there's always a showdown it seems. High noon can happen anywhere. I like to think of high noon as that moment when just the vibe you radiate as a femme fatale chrome cowgal is enough to make even dust settle and rise on command.

Road Diary:

On course for the two-and-half-day jaunt to my favorite rally, Sturgis. I made it in record time to Cedar Shore Resort. It's right on the Missouri River. I can see thunderstorms ranting and raving across the water, while all is clear and lovely on the west side where I am. It rained pretty good here the night before. The ground is soft but I don't care. I'm tickled to be here and setting up camp on the embankment. A big block of wood under the kickstand will keep Tigerlily from spilling over into the mud. The evening air is intoxicatingly fresh. I feel like I have bionic smelling abilities from so many hours in the saddle. It rained a little today, but I didn't care. It was refreshing . . . I just kept on riding. I stumbled upon the Christian Motorcycle Association's Biker Aid Station coming north through Iowa. Apparently Jesse James had ridden through there the day before. They were excited about that. I'm excited about Jesse, too. A handsome, tattooed American craftsman and artist, who wouldn't be? As soon as I pulled in to gas up, they handed me a bottle of water and cleaned my windshield. They found that I'm a Jesus lover, so they offered up prayer. It was a nice prayer about safety and all. About being protected. I thought about my own prayer that I needed to say . . . let me choose the best direction in life.

Off they sent me with a bottle of trial-size Purel to sanitize my grubby road hands. I'd pour it on my head, too, if I could to get rid of any stinkin' thinkin'. That's what I love about the road so much. . . . It clears the head and brings about the best thinking. Because out here, there's just no other way to be but happy and free. No matter what.

I'm beginning to like this feeling of being missed by someone special. Wow, I have someone to come home to who understands my gypsy soul, a dude who encourages my artistic self, who wants me to always be just me. He wants me out here discovering things and thinking things through. How amazing to think I've got a warm hug to snuggle into at the end of my trip. His arms and a snuggle with my kitty GypZ Jingles. Yeah, after all these years of being single, hmm. . . . He's a good soul, a good companion. I think I like that kinda route in my life. And root.

Mean People Suck Alerts

* Cigarettes thrown out the window from the vehicle in front of you.

* Folks on cell phones who cut you off or make left turns in front of you.

* Pedestrians who stride in front of a moving motorcycle as if it were a bicycle, able to stop on immediate command.

* Hotel clerks who refuse rooms to bikers.

* New motorcycle riders who try to behave like outlaw bad asses with their attitude mugs on while they pass you by and leave you stranded on the side of the road.

* Being served old coffee that's been sitting for hours because you look like you can't even pay for a cup.

* Catty females who judge you because of your eccentric road style and odd motorcycle choice.

* Being told by a boy that girls shouldn't ride motorcycles.

* A boss who tells you that you can't go on your motorcycle vacation at the last minute. Yeah, right.

* Media and entertainment industry people who treat all chick bikers like their own manifested Hollywood image of a leather-clad ditz. We are sexy, powerful, and free!

* Overpriced motorcycle labor and parts, and dishonest technicians who try to outsmart a female rider. Last laugh on that chump.

* A motorcycle salesman who treats a female customer as invisible or ignorant. There's power in pink . . . ever hear of a pink slip?

* Anybody who makes you try to feel bike shame, as in, your bike's not good enough or cool enough or pretty enough. Phooey.

* Anybody who tries to hold you back from realizing your dreams or makes you feel less than the powerhouse talent that you really are! You are a star!

* People who park for extra-long periods of time at the gas station pump while they enjoy a pee stop and coffee in the convenience store.

* People who tell you to grow up. Also tag them with a superhero Band-Aid.

* Squids, newbee riders who selfishly ride recklessly, endangering the lives of other motorists.

MEAN PEOPLE SUCK

There are people you'll meet on the open road who are mean. And mean people suck. What you need to do when you meet a mean person is not spoil your headspace with anger or any other negative thing. You just want to call it as you see it. I suggest you supply yourself with a bunch of little red stickers that say "mean people suck" and then you *tag* that mean person if you're able to with that sticker somewhere on their person or vehicle. Or you send them intense kindness vibes and kill them with kindness.

CHROME COWGIRL INSPIRATION

When I started riding, I'd see the other Chrome Cowgirls out there who inspired me with their swagger and confidence. It was great to witness. They thrive within the motorcycle culture, and their passion for riding carves their dream paths and helps them through the tough times. They have that high-octane confidence and beauty most of the time, no matter what they're doing in their everyday lives.

* Among those who inspire me is Motorcycle Hall of Famer, author, and motojournalist, Cris Sommer-Simmons, with her long hair flowing along with her pen, saddled on a vintage Harley that she could fix herself. Just reading her work and watching her on television made me realize that it would be okay for me to let my art come forth without apology. She's truly a vision of the free-spirited yet grounded Chrome Cowgirl with a lovely family.
* Same with my friend Malysa Wyse, who didn't give a crap what anyone thought when she posed for *Playboy,* the first real biker chick to do that. Body and bike are art to her; therefore her editorial was about the truth and beauty of riding and loving the wind, the naked truth. She took her message around the globe and proudly led rides and gave autograph sessions.
* Some modern heroines include Athena of Vagabond Choppers, who knows how to ration bike parts and resourcefully fabricate interesting pieces on her custom choppers while she's juggling

TRIP TIP

Tipping big is sexy.

Chrome Cowgirl Calamity Betz gives her Wild West perspective on saddling up and galloping beyond the comfort zone

If you're not standing on the edge, then you are missing the view. The view of what? The view of life. I like to live my life on the edge of my own comfort zone. Why? Comfort is something we all enjoy. It feels good to stay in our comfort zones, whatever that is, doesn't it? It feels good to be curled up in our favorite spots, with our dogs next to us, watching our favorite TV shows, bowls of popcorn in our laps. But there is such an amazing world out there! Have you been watching Discovery Channel's "Planet Earth"? Have you read *National Geographic's* book that portrays every country in the world? Good God, there is so much to do and see that I don't know if there will be time!

I push myself to the edge of my own comfort zone so that I will find all of my own limitations. I try to push myself to be the best I can be with what resources God has given me. I want to explore every path that God leads me down, and leave no stone unturned. I believe that he gives me the lessons I am to learn, and the experiences that I am to have, and the people that I am to know. I try *not* to ignore whatever is put in my path.

Whether I like it or not, I try to get as much as possible out of every experience I am given. Even the ones where I am secretly asking God, "What in the hell have you brought me to this place for?" Because I believe there is a reason.

I am a biker chick, and sometimes I am rough around the edges. I make a lot of stupid mistakes, and have suffered many failures. What has made me the strong woman I am is my ability to laugh at myself. To try again, and again, and to keep believing thru it all.

I do have fear, but what I have that makes me stronger than the fear is faith. I believe in God, and Jesus, and Heaven. I am not afraid of where I am going, so I am unafraid to live boldly. If there is a dream in my heart and soul, I will pursue it. If that makes no sense to anyone on earth but myself, does that matter? At the end of this journey, I believe you answer to one person, and one person only. And in my opinion, believing in your creator is believing in yourself. It's one and the same, and one cannot fully happen without the other. Being a true warrior is learning to be true to yourself, in every moment.

the role of mom and entrepenuer, running a motorcycle shop with her hubby.

★ Betsy Huelskamp, my wonderful windsister and beloved riding companion, is an absolutely radiant source of inspiration with her free spirit soaring, her hand held high making a peace sign and yelling "Wahoo!" as she speeds down the freeway on her rusted custom Harley-Davidson chopper. What a force these ladies are to every woman around the globe.

For me, riding a motorcycle is like going to church. This land is His land, this land is our land. And when you are out on the open road, everything around you is a gift, and a miracle. The mountains, the deserts, the rivers and wildlife. It's where I go to do my thinking, my talking, and my connecting to that which is bigger than myself. It clears my mind to go on a long road trip, and puts the little problems into better perspective.

Riding a motorcycle is better than any therapy you could ever hope for. Only you know what is in your own heart. But sometimes life has a way of tangling you in your own cobwebs. Riding in the wind can blow those old stagnant webs away and give you a fresh outlook. It's not going to solve your problems; you still have to do that. But it will give you the added strength and courage you need for whatever it is that lies ahead! In the words of the late, great John Wayne, "Courage is being scared to death, but saddling up anyway."

So saddle up!

—Betsy "Calamity Betz" Huelskamp, a dear friend, windsister, and co-star of *Motorcycle Women* on the Discovery Channel

★ Jasmine Cain is a motorcycle songstress. She is a great example of doing things her way, blazing trails, and hanging tough, combining her showdown style with her unstoppable artistry. She honed her musical craft performing for hundreds of thousands of riders at motorcycle rallies and rodeos across the country. She embodies the true cowgirl, having grown up on a ranch, and her Chrome Cowgirl spirit lassos the heart of the motorcycle rider with her high-octane music.

* JoAnn Bortles lays down the law with her bad-ass class attitude. She loves her art and her passion for motorcycles. No boy would walk into her shop and tell her how her shop should be run because there would be a showdown. She defined how her paint business was gonna run in a man's motorcycle world, and twenty-eight years later, she's laughing all the way down the highway on her custom chopper with her dreams coming true.

* And then there's Sara Liberte, with a passion for wrenching on bikes and viewing the world as art—taking her camera with her everywhere she goes to capture the soulful moments that happen in the motorcycle culture and business.

* Vivian "Gypsy" Charros took the prize as the first biker chick to ever win a Discovery Channel *Biker Build-Off* with her Bitch Slap bike, a bad-ass beauty indeed.

* Sam Morgan, a fine artist, lets everyone know that a woman on a motorcycle defies gravity as she stunt rides on the Wall of Death MotorDrome with a huge smile.

* Angelle (Savoie) Sampey, oh, she let the boys know who's da boss of the nitro drag races. She is truly inspired by the little sticker on her windshield that is her mantra: "I can do all things through Christ who strengthens me" (Philippians 4:13). And zoom, she's off and leading the competition.

* My favorite legendary riders are Effie and Avis Hotchkiss from Brooklyn, a mother and daughter team who rode cross-country in 1915 on a Harley, daughter commanding the motorcycle, mom tucked in the sidecar knitting away.

* The coolest motorcycle club is the Motor Maids, among others, and is the oldest female motorcycle riding club in North America.

The culture thrives with powerful female riders who ride their own style of life and inspire women the world over to really claim their lives and move through fear. Having a bright, sassy attitude is the foundation for being an all-American, all-girl motorcycling bad ass.

My life preserver generally is to pray for safety on the road. But this rather tall, steely Smith & Wesson certainly could ward off any type of predator. *Author's note: This gun is not loaded. It's nearly half my size and scary, eh?* Carlos Torres

Lassoing the road. *Dennis Curnette*

Lift your wings and ride.

— *Motor City Angels, Detroit, MI*

Route 3
ROADACIOUS
U Own the Road

The Chrome Cowgirl claims her road. She claims her lane, her destiny, her life's journey. That is being roadacious in life. What does it mean to own your road? When you first begin riding or racing or dirt biking, whenever you embark upon a journey, there is a hesitation, and then all these fretful thoughts happen.

But that initial spark that ignited your desire to move past your comfort zone is still there glowing ever brighter.

"Own your road" is what a pioneering female rider once told me. She's a trucker, too, and an Iron Butt rider (www.ironbutt.com— The World's Toughest Motorcycle Competition) who rides all the saddle-sore showdown miles. What she meant by that is: protect

Even as a small tot I wandered the open roads looking for adventure.

yourself, ride with confidence. You're the boss of the two-wheeled experience that you've embarked upon . . . so own it.

The Chrome Cowgirl knows when she's got to saddle up and find another way, another path to her dreams. She'll fashion an opportunity if she can't find any. Another road to a solution may be just around the bend, and she has got to *vroom* through the twists and turns to find it. We Chrome Cowgirls stay in that saddle no matter what and lasso a new direction if we don't like the old one. So my dear windsisters, saddle up! We are cowgirls, only we ride chrome.

Shut Up and Ride How To's

* *Wise up*. Take a Motorcycle Safety course and get your license. It's fun to learn from a friend. A boyfriend might show you everything not to do because he loves to wrestle with his ride, but you need to get the straight truth. I know you don't want to hurt anyone's feelings, especially someone who is sure he can teach you, but if you let a friend teach you, you will pick up all his or her bad habits. You'll miss the whole flow of learning the right way. The motorcycle classes provide everything you need, including a practice bike on which to learn, a helmet, the written test, and the driving test. After that, hey, take an advanced class, too. Then you can teach your boyfriend a thing or two about riding. The more you know about riding, the more fun it is because you'll be the queen of the road.

* *Gear up*. Get awesome, pretty motorcycle gear that's functional for riding. Heavy-duty jacket, gloves, boots, helmet, eyewear, fleece neck warmer, flashy lipstick. Gearing up for the ride is a thrill . . . and it's fun to wear your leathers even when you're not riding. Show off your leather-clad, beautiful self! Be seen!

* *Get fit*. Find a bike that feels comfortable and manageable and make it fit you by changing out the handlebars, adjusting the foot and hand controls, and changing the seat if need be. Just wait until you indulge yourself on all the choices that are out there.

* *Power practice*. Practice riding around your neighborhood, read books on motorcycling, and watch training DVDs. Take advanced classes if you can. Ride within your skill level at all times. Learn to ride all kinds of styles (racing, dirt, motocross, advanced street). It is so much fun to learn new things and then apply these nuggets of knowledge on a long ride. Don't forget to share what you know, too!

* *Get saddle time*. Find some great riding organizations and groups to ride with so that you can meet other cool riders and build up your riding abilities. Get out there and have ridelicious fun on solo voyages, too.

* *Have fun, relax, and laugh a lot!*

For me, riding a motorcycle is like breathing. It's part of what keeps me alive. Having spent 28 years in the custom motorcycle business, I have seen so very much. . . . And to appreciate just how far we have come, you only have to look back and be amazed at the long road that many women in this business had to travel.

— JoAnn Bortles, Crazy Horse Painting; author, journalist, custom bike designer

GET LOST SO YOU CAN BE FOUND: SOULO

It's all about you on the ride. End of story. So get lost. Forget about all the who, what, when, why, and how of life and just get out there and wander. A Chrome Cowgirl loves to get lost in the moment and let the experience carry her through. You have an idea about the outcome of the trip. You sort of know you're going to Sturgis, but you may push past that and end up in Thermopolis, Wyoming, before you head back home.

Keep your curiosity alive. All that programming you acquired from your experiences—you know, the inner naysayers from days gone by that still linger—it don't exist. Blown out like a water hose blasting a spider web. Riding is your moment to get lost from what you know and how you think things ought to be. Sometimes you just have to surrender to that "which way should I go?" moment.

Because down the road filled with unknowns is a most spectacular experience to be had. But you wouldn't know it if you were afraid to get lost in the wilds of intuition. You know nothing out there on the open road; you become an empty canvas. Let the road teach you to be a pioneer. If you let yourself get lost out there, wandering the great wide-open roads knowing nothing, you'll find a power will emerge within you and intuition will lead your way.

TRIP TIP
People driving cars are blind. They never see motorcycles, so make sure you are living and riding out loud. Be seen! Wear bright colors and get crafty with reflective tape, and avoid riding in other drivers' blind spots.

Long distance riding has changed my life by giving me a positive attitude. Life throws many things at us, most of which we are in no position to change, so the only thing we can do is have the proper attitude.

— *Phyllis Lang, Iron Butt Rally veteran*

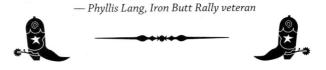

I-DENT-A-TEE. WHO R U?

Every Chrome Cowgirl is glorious and powerful in her own way. Each one of us is definitely a shut-up-and-ride kind of gal. There's no time for excuses, only time to ride free and live life to the fullest. Because your life is waiting. Remember, time waits for no one and nothing. There's no time like *now* . . . so make sure you revisit the definition of "ridelicious time."

Chrome Cowgirls ignore the opinions of others when it impinges upon their free will. They saddle up close to their own hearts and souls once they realize they have an incredible gift, available to everyone: the freedom to be. *Hallelujah!* Free will is a favor from God. And we're all favored, see. Most of us have no idea what to do with this lovely bonus from the almighty universal creator. Free will is the gas that makes your bike and life go, go, go. Free will is gas that makes your whole life open into this vast expanse of possibility, of hope, of dreams, of sanctity. Free will is the equivalent of flying in your dreams. It is the will to exercise your freedom, to soar. Riding is the equivalent of what it's like to fly in your dreams, with the wind rushing past you as you're weightless and invincible, flexible, and adaptable! Only with riding, that feeling of flying is real, not a dream.

Riding gives you wings. A Chrome Cowgirl lives by this creed. It's like the motorcycle is her unicorn. In the beautiful wind is that sound that rushes around us like the wings of a thousand angels guiding us at each mile. A lot of times folks have no idea that their souls have

Flying along the highway on my Harley is to soar so high that I can kiss the sky.

wings to fly. But there are certain moments and experiences that will unfold those wings. One moment you will be flapping clumsily and the next soaring higher and higher, traveling far and wide. At such moments you become aware of your surroundings, of your breath, of every moment that your free will is unleashed, and there ain't no turnin' back to what was. Because what was ain't no more.

Free will provides you with the means to discover your identity, your truth, untainted by opinions and outside influences. And what more delightful way to discover your own truth than on a motorcycle?

Let's have a peek at some of the Chrome Cowgirl personalities. You may be a combination of several of these personality types.

Lift Your Wings and Ride!

— *Motor City Angels, Detroit, Michigan,*
an all-girl motorcycle club

Chopper Gypsy

The Chopper Gypsy is ol' skool meets new; she's a hippie, biker gypsy. An artist and a lover of service, she's extremely free-spirited and certainly walks to the beat of a different drummer. This vibrant chixie doesn't dress or look like a typical biker chick. She doesn't let the dumb ass judgments of others get to her sweet, vagabond soul. A definition of "free to be herself," she dresses like a cross between a Native American princess and a rockabilly chick. Tattoos tell her story. Piercings may adorn her belly and nose. Her way of life is all about peace, love, and riding. The perfect date for her might be dinner at a truck stop with a charming wayward male who's saddled on his own ride. Her rain gear might be to roll her bike under an underpass after she's gotten a pretty good soak. She'll wear plastic sacks on her feet to keep 'em dry and wear wool leg warmers over road-worn leather pants to keep warm. Against all odds, she'll venture out into the night to ride the highways with the big wheelers under a full moon, which serves as an additional headlight. Chopper Gypsy camps out willingly and will also pull her bike under an overhang and find rest on a select piece of on-sale patio furniture displayed in front of a department store. She's nature's wild child—like a cheetah on the run charging across the asphalt. A colorful character, her world is a kaleidoscope of possibility, and she'll earn her way across the country if she must. Her motorcycle is a rolling piece of artwork, chopped out front and decorated with odds and ends, treasures she may have found on the road or at a yard sale, or maybe from a random thrift

To be ourselves causes us to be exiled by many others, and yet to comply with what others want causes us to be exiled from ourselves.

— *Clarissa Pinkola Estés, author of*
Women Who Run With Wolves

I roar down the road like a tiger and ride the breeze soft as a lily. *Robert Smith*

shop. Sometimes she wrenches her own ride because she's curious about the inner soul, the inner roar of the motorcycle and will tear it apart for further investigation. Much to the chagrin of motorcycle safety advocates, Chopper Gypsy doesn't like to wear a helmet, and if she must, she will decorate her helmet with all kinds of art media and then wear it like a prized cowgirl hat.

Racey Jane

Got a need for speed? For dragging your knee around the track? Are you addicted to the types of hairpins that you ride through on your bike instead of slide into your hair? Racey Jane is about competition. Leading the pack. This super hero is alpha girl, for sure. Dressed in a full leather racing suit, Racey Jane burns up tracks and loves to seize a lane, make it all hers. Adrenaline pumps through her veins as she plays catch-me-if-you-can when she leaps off the starting line. The shriek of high-performance engines battling it out on the asphalt is music to her ears. The smell of gasoline and hot asphalt is her perfume. Her racer riding style is about sheer determination and focus. This Chrome Cowgirl is highly goal oriented: to win, or at the very least, be better. Like a cat, every move she makes is carefully executed, carefully thought through with a result to achieve ... absolute excellence in performance. And to prove her riding skills are worth a salt, Racey Jane will rev her throttle and roll at lightning speed across the baking hot salt flats, peppering others with uncontainable laughter upon achieving her winning score. This fast girl will tweak the performance of her own ride and is proud of her tune-up kit. She'll fine-tune her ride of life and rake the competition over the asphalt coals. The pit is her bed of roses.

May we all grow old with most of our limbs attached.

— Erika Lopez, author, actress, screenwriter,
multi-media fine artist

Road Diary:

I don't claim to be any kind of authority on the concept of freedom because freedom is a definition of the individual's soul. Like a drink of water to parched lips, souls around the globe crave freedom. Freedom can be elusive, though. To be free is to have faith. It's rollin' with the flow. Up 'til this morning, it was clear riding ahead. Crisp blue skies and hot sun. Lots of clarity and now I'm in a fog. I know the sunrise is out there somewhere over the Missouri River. Last night, a wet, low ceiling of clouds moved in, blurring the ground with the sky. I didn't have enough celebratory drink last night to be distortedly hung over . . . so yeah, this was a weather thing.

The scene outside my wet tent looks like an artist decided to white their canvas and start their painting all over again. I crawl out of my tent after sitting awhile experiencing the dampness settle in my bones. Oh, I crave a strong, thick coffee, but I need to pack up and go. Sloppy, soupy ground . . . it rained pretty good, too. My awesome orange and blue tent now is brown with blades of grass stuck to it like a chocolate cupcake with green sprinkles. I manage to roll her up and stick her in the sack and the wet bungee task begins. I put everything in black garbage bags. They're the best if you can't afford the fancy tour packs and accessories. I sort of like the gypsy look anyway. "You git yourself them heavy duty black garbage bags and put yer belongin's in there darlin' and you won't have no trouble with the rain gettin' in your stuff again," Brother Speed once told me. It was early and one of those oh-jeez-I-don't-want-to-wake-up-the-whole-campground-by-starting-my-bike moments. Tigerlily rumbled to life. She was way jonesing for the road, looking forward to wandering through the Badlands together.

I was hoping that this was one of those fogs that burns away instead of just lifting up a bit so it can get a good aim to rain on your parade with those bullet-sting rain drops. "Ha Ha, take this little rider. How hard you gonna hang in there now?" Weather that storm, I always say.

I took a two-mile jaunt over to hang out at Al's Oasis, where everybody's got smiling faces, and grabbed a coffee. Disappointingly watery. It became beige water once the milk swirled into it. The lot was packed with bikes on route to Sturgis and moody bikers dressed in rain gear. Nobody likes to ride in the rain, especially wearing nerdy rain gear that makes you feel like sausage meat stuffed in a skin. My nerdy gear featured bandanas tied around my calves and ankles to keep the wind from puffing me up. It made the outfit look a bit more fashionista and unique, too. Somewhere I want to get a funky rubber belt with decorative beer and soda caps on it to fasten down the jacket so I don't look like a sumo wrestler when that wind balloons the rain gear into wind sails.

Standing still, it's really not raining. That changes when you get in the wind. Then it's like those clouds are wringing themselves out on you. A few miles up the road and, dude, I was socked in and the rain gear was doing its job keeping me dry while streaks of water wiggled up the nylon pant legs. Eight yellow dashes was all I could manage to see ahead of me. I slowed down on the 75-mile-an-hour stretch. Way down. I passed a lot of boys in packs, this solo girl did, oh yes. (I just love that. VaVaVaVroom . . . on my chopped out little Sportster with my ass hurting on my sexy seat with no support, feeling like I'm being jack hammered by the road.)

Oh I'd pass those boys and then they would disappear in my side mirror as if the clouds sucked them in. Riding in this fog, I felt an odd comfort, a sort of cozy calm and foreboding at the same time. You see, I had to have faith that there wasn't a large critter standing in the road or some other nightmare surprise lurking in the foggy shadows. I had faith, wind whispering faith. It was like riding in a womb.

I knew that the sunlight was going to burn off the gray density. The scent was a combination of wet grass and farming. At times through the gray there'd be this silver glow as if the sun were a flashlight atop a sheet, but it just couldn't shine through all the way yet. The horizon would look bright, brighter, bright, and then dull again. And then suddenly the sun would break full on through, a mere puzzle piece of sky with white clouds ghosting the rays, then it would be gone again. So I coached the sun: Come on, you can do it! It seemed to get warmer in that fog; I knew the sun was closing in to erase the fog. It seemed to take hours, but when the skies were clear, I emerged feeling like a Goddess.

The Real World: The Feminine Face of God. This was inspired by my motorcycle journeys. Your goddess will emerge once you shut up and ride, and you will have command over your world! *Road-inspired art by Sasha*

Follow your Grandmother Moon.
Her illuminating cycles will transform your spirit.

— Lakota Sioux

**Her symbol is water—like the fog all around us.
The Goddess uses water as the means
to manifest Herself.**

— from Paulo Coelho's By the River Piedra
I Sat Down and Wept

Earthy Chick

It's mud, guts, and glory for this girl. She loves challenging terrain.
Give her the opportunity to jump high and freestyle over a challenging
mound of earth and she's all about it. Like a Cirque du Soleil bird in
flight, she and her freestyle bike will glide like an eagle and land as
precisely as a hawk on prey as the tires grip the earth. Earthy Chick
may also tango her motorcycle in a competitive dance of trials, for
an extreme test of skill. She'll jump at the chance of an endurance
challenge, with a desire to prove to the world that she can endure
the most impossible course upon Mother Earth. Earthy Chick loves
to get down and dirty on her motorcycle and become one with the
mud. Don't cross her on the motocross circuit because she will leave
you in the dust. This girl might get a broken arm or broken leg from
her environmental motorcycle endeavors, but her spirit can never be
broken. This dirty lifestyle is joyfully shared between mothers and
children of all ages.

Iron Godiva

Iron Godiva is all about the distance. She's all about building
a custom from the ground up. She's the goddess, sword drawn,
ready to defend and protect all that is ridelicious. She is a mighty
Aphrodite, a Venus rising from a silken pool of hot chrome. To her,
riding is an aphrodisiac. It's intoxicating. Seductive. Distance is
her drug. Such the creatoress, she'll birth her motorcycle from the
ground up, selecting its ingredients like a gourmet recipe to build a

Motorcycle Metamorphosis
OPTIMISTIC LIFESTYLE CHANGES THAT HAPPEN WHEN YOU RIDE A MOTORCYCLE

★ *Outlook:* You acquire a fresh perspective about self and thoughts about self, as if you're an outsider meeting yourself for the first time and you're eager to learn more.

★ *Acceptance:* You become accepting of yourself because you realize that you're precious and amazingly cool and unique exactly as you are. Bonus things will happen, too; for instance, you will suddenly not care about cellulite.

★ *Victory:* You feel lots of little personal victories during and after every magical motorcycle journey, even during the most challenging moments.

★ *Uplifting:* You can throttle your frown upside down, and you glow with a smile so wide that if you were eating an ear of corn, you'd have kernels in your ears.

★ *Confidence:* You learn to let go of preconceived anythings and everythings, and you end up riding farther and reaching beyond those boundaries of fear and uncertainty. You want to try new things and dump old crappy things that don't work in life.

★ *Wholeness:* You feel a wholeness about yourself because the hole that you felt has been filled with wind whispering angels inspiring you to be true to your desires and goals, and to maximize the God-given blessings that are your treasures in the world.

★ *Personal security:* You only want to travel your own road, and you don't concern yourself with what everybody else is doing. You don't concern yourself with what others think about you.

★ *Community:* You gain a bunch of new friends from all walks in life. People who you'd never expect even to say hello to in a grocery store become family members for life because you share a love for riding motorcycles.

★ *Retreat:* Riding a motorcycle becomes a moving retreat that becomes an almost insatiable craving.

★ *Stillness:* You experience a beautiful stillness in your soul while you roll along, and it feels like everything is going to be okay no matter what. In that stillness are the ultimate tools for problem solving. Be still and know.

★ *Thrive:* Away from routine your soul can thrive, and the good thing about riding a motorcycle is that it is always available to take you away from the routine.

★ *Charity:* You want to encourage those less fortunate. You realize that life is terribly short, and there is no time like the present to be a gift to another and give of yourself.

★ *Renew:* You can sit on the bike even in the winter and just feel the soul of the bike merge with yours and all those sweet road memories just pour right back all fresh and new, renewing your soul.

masterpiece. She seeks to fill her garage with tools and motorcycles. A queen of the highway, the Iron Godiva will ride five hundred miles or more chasing the sunset and following the sunrise. Under a ceiling of stars, she'll whisk along the roads and sleep under that illuminated canvas or sink soft into a warm bed on her journey. The Iron Godiva is prepared; she's maternal and nurtures the journey, coaxes the road experiences forth. You may see her dressed head to toe in an Aerostich riding suit or in sleek expensive leathers and all-matching accessories. "No" is not an option in her book. Attitude is everything to the Iron Godiva. She is determined to go the distance or to finish a build no matter what it takes. The Iron Godiva loves a touring machine, whether it's American-made or from another land. She embodies what it means to go the distance. A robust tour bike affords her luxuriously long distance and creature comforts necessary for a long journey. She's ready, willing, and able, and there's no road too long, too uncharted, too lumpy, or too winding for this saddle-loving rider. Iron Godiva loves steel and looks quite at home behind a welding mask.

Foxy Rider
Glam girl. Gorgeous and cunning like one of Charlie's Angels. She's keen on checking out the scenarios that she rides through as if it's a magical mystery tour. Perhaps folks are amazed when they find out this femme fatale is a Chrome Cowgirl. She's far from the stereotypes. Foxy Rider's so, well, subtle as she roams around the countryside. Whether beautiful inside or outside or both, she glows with the road. Sometimes she rides solo, and sometimes she rides with a pack of fabulous girl-power riders. She rarely knows the meaning of helmet head, since her locks seem perfectly coifed beneath her lid. The Foxy Rider will saddle up on a vintage classic bike, perhaps telling you everything you'd ever want to know about that particular model. She's obsessed with details and drinks the knowledge of the culture, the technology behind the ride. Lipstick is her friend, and you may find her dismounting and quickly applying a fresh coat, picking out the bugs and wiping away the grime as fast as could be. She's clever as a fox and great at outsmarting. You may

discover this Foxy Rider is also a motorcycle safety instructor. She loves to teach, to guide, to demonstrate the finesse of riding. There is no unteachable student out there as far as she's concerned. To the Foxy Rider, just learn to ride. It is a life lesson. She is the three "B"s: brains, beauty, biker.

The Chrome Cowgirl ABCs to Live By

POST THIS LIST ANY PLACE YOU NEED QUICK INSPIRATION DURING THOSE DAYS OF PMS

(PARKED MOTORCYCLE SYNDROME)

A—ATTITUDE. Riding a motorcycle inspires a positive can-do attitude.

B—BOHEMIAN. Set loose your inner biker bohemian, proudly ignoring conventional standards and one routine, and embark upon a journey with not an ounce of structure to it.

C—COURAGE. It takes courage to saddle up on a motorcycle alone, while it is leaking oil, and head to an awesome rally somewhere with only $75.00 in your pocket.

D—DARING. A modest bit of fear creeps in while on a journey, but that daring spirit is a reminder that it is great to be alive on the ride.

E—EMPOWERING. We ride motorcycles because riding is empowering; it kick-starts life, revving up every aspect of simply existing.

F—FANTASTIC. When my co-workers ask, "Why are you taking a whole lunch hour and riding a motorcycle?" I respond, "Because it's fantastic. It's my food for thought. It satisfies my cravings; it relieves my voracious appetite." Fantastic also describes how I look and feel in my riding gear.

G—GIGGLE. Giggle is what you do when you ride a motorcycle. Even when you're feeling blue there bubbles to the surface a giggle, encouraged by your bike tickling your heart.

H—HEAVENLY. A word often used to describe a riding experience when nothing else will do.

I—INCREDIBLE. A word to utter nonstop while cruising wild and free through many different landscapes.

J—JOURNEY. To ditch life as you know it, to follow the heartfelt journey in a way that is possible only on a motorcycle.

K—KISMET. To hear that engine roar to life and to ease that clutch out, launching you on the first mile of a journey, is pure kismet.

L—LOVE. The female motorcycle rider is a giant love magnet, in love with herself, in love with her friends and family, in love with life, in love with the art of the journey.

M—MAGICAL. To ride a motorcycle is to live breath to breath and moment to moment with eyes on the horizon ahead—and there lies the simply magical.

KEEP YOUR EYE ON THE HORIZON PRIZE: CHASING DREAMS AND IDENTIFYING GOALS

Everybody's got dreams and goals. Some of those goals seem like they have drifted so far away, it's near impossible to hook and reel 'em back home to you. But they are there, closer than you

N—NATURE. Without the confines of an automotive cage, you're more exposed to the presence of Mother Nature and the call of the wild that makes you *roarrr* through life!

O—OBSERVE. Observe everything in a most supernatural way inspired by a motorcycle high.

P—PROMISING. Chasing a horizon while riding two wheels always leads to a promising experience.

Q—QUALITY. Riding provides a generous boost in the quality of one's life.

R—RECHARGE. The high-voltage current of divine change will jolt through you to recharge the very core of your being while you're rolling down the road. No doubt about it, you feel recharged when you return home from your magical mystery motorcycle camping tour.

S—SACRED. Alone in the canyon, you hear the wind-whispering angels confirm that, yes, the motorcycle will guide you to that sacred place.

T—TENACIOUS. The Chrome Cowgirl is tenacious, which keeps her hardcore riding on the road of her destiny.

U—UTOPIA. Riding away from mediocrity, you ride toward sheer utopia.

V—VALOR. Your valor is in accepting your voluptuous self: The cool curves of your hips and personality. The fullness of your unique perspective. The well-endowed depths of your soul.

W—WILLING. The Chrome Cowgirl is willing to ride the extra hundred miles so that she can experience Salt Lake at sundown. Ready? Willing? Then start your engine!

X—XANADU. Sturgis, South Dakota, is a rider's Xanadu.

Y—YEARNING. Behind the fabric walls of her secretary cubicle, she had an insatiable yearning to race her Suzuki Gixxer at Laguna Seca.

Z—ZEAL. Her zeal for riding her motorcycle 500 miles per day was impressive.

I'm most happy and free to be chasing the horizon of my dreams, and you can, too! Go for it! *Michael Lichter*

think, waiting to be recognized. While you're a busybody with all kinds of activities, you put the dreams and goals on the back burner. Well, go get them. You'll find them waiting for you on the horizon, vivid and glowing. Those dreams are meant to be captured by you.

Motorcycle riding leads you right smack to those dreams and goals. A motorcycle not only delivers you there, that two-wheeled machine mysteriously empowers you to follow your destiny. Then you can't help but take the reigns and make things happen.

A motorcycle is the vehicle that allows you to be yourself, because you were born to be . . .

Dream it, see it, you can achieve it! Never quit! My inspiration for going the distance is faith in God, myself, and the loved ones who support my passion.

— Female motorcyclist DJ Jones became the first person to ride the same motorcycle through all 50 states, September 2006

Waiting for things to happen in a passive manner doesn't exist anymore. The pioneering Chrome Cowgirl gallops deep into her motoadventure to bring her dreams to life. She owns her road, and there isn't another driver alive who will take her lane. Never does she take her eye far from the horizon, where hope lives and possibility is aglow.

I'm a dreamer. The dictionary definition of a dreamer includes: 1. visionary; 2. idealist. The other definition is: "habitually impractical person." Well, all right, then! Because I say, under whose definition am I that? People constantly tag situations as impractical because they may not fit into routine, or known practices, or are highly unusual. People who love the adventure that comes with the pursuit of dreams may very well be considered "habitual" in their attempts to ride off into the sunset to enjoy yet another dream ride on two wheels. A set of loud pipes to announce, "Yeah, we're here to dream and chase the dreams in our hearts!" This could be deemed impractical, but so be it! A dreamer! Habitually impractical!

Chrome Cowgirls are pioneers; they are visionaries and idealists, and that's awesome because a Chrome Cowgirl makes dreams happen. Everything good happens on a motorcycle. She saddles up on her chrome horse and rides off into the dawn of a new, dreamy day filled with hope, inspiration, and faith, living life full throttle. To be a wild dreamer requires action on those dreams. A real dreamer couples action with her great vision.

I love riding with the wind on my face because it lets me feel free from the constraints of everyday life. I encourage all those restless women out there to take up the challenge to roar and ride!

— *Mandie Crawford, president, Roaring Women Ltd.*

The perfect cruising posture is when you're sitting up straight, arms wide on the handlebars as if you're about to embrace the sun. *Road-inspired art by Sasha.*

FUEL FOR THOUGHT

The motorcycle is the flow. That's why we girls are so great at riding motorcycles. We know about the flow, the cycle of life. But sometimes with all the demands on us we lose who we are. That's a saving grace moment. Recognizing the M.E. (My Experience). If you ride away from all you know and let the wanderlust inside of you lead the way, that's rollin' with the flow. Whatever happens becomes a cool chapter in the book of your life. If you say, "It's time for a little impromptu livin'," then you're ready to roll with the flow. No fear. Shimmy down the road in wanderlust style.

Everything good happens on a motorcycle!

The motorcycle becomes an extension of your body.

— *Sara Liberte, RT's North Hills Cycle, Inc.*

Route 4
MOTOCURE
Manicures for the Motorcycle, Mind, and Mood

Motorcycling is a mind-altering experience. The sport is a mood enhancer. People get high from riding because two-wheeled scootin' is about two-wheeled shootin' down the highway. Smokin' in the turns. Poppin' wheelies. Cookin' the road. You become comfortably bum with all your senses rocked. Out there on the open road, rolling with the flow, suddenly life will present you with *life*. And you will be high on life.

Maintaining your wonderful bike keeps that mood up. It's peace of mind. The motorcycle likes to be groomed and highly maintained because it wants to go the distance. It wants to be fast and show its stuff. It wants to have horsepower for its Chrome Cowgirl. Like the Pony Express, it wants to deliver the goods. Always remember that your life depends on the condition of the machine, whether it is the motorcycle or the way you maintain your own health.

What's in your toolbox?

TOOLS FOR THE ROAR: LIFE TOOLS— HOW TO WRENCH, REPAIR, MAINTAIN

A Chrome Cowgirl has some great life tools:

- ★ She embraces change.
- ★ She lives from the heart.
- ★ She is compassionate.
- ★ She has boundaries.
- ★ She's action oriented.
- ★ She's cowgirl tough!

Moving through different environments and landscapes places the Chrome Cowgirl in some fun scenarios. Staying in one place is boring and way too routine. Change is good. It's great, in fact. Altering the course of direction almost always leads to some unpredictable yet thrilling experience. It might not always be fun, but the episode makes a great road story. Motorcycle riding equals change. The creature-comfort ratio pales in comparison to that of a fully equipped car, but that's so boring. The change that happens when you ride includes everything from change in the weather and change in direction to change in your attitude and change in your style. It's all about staying loose and changing. Loose change. *Roll with the flow.*

Some changes that happen within the first week of riding

DIRECTION	Bound and determined to visit your friend in Idaho, you've got average miles calculated, stops factored in, and timing considered.	"*I da hoped* I'd get to my friend's house by now, but I decided to take the back road and then relax in a hot spring. What day is it?" No time like the PRESENT.
STYLE	Perfect riding gear, not a bug splat on the leathers, everything matches (including your lipstick), and your hair is smoothed back into a slick ponytail. You're lookin' all business.	Your helmet has stickers declaring your independence all over it, your leathers are pitted with bug kill, you have your virgin motorcycle voyage date tattooed on your wrist, and your hair is braided with beads and leather strips. A few dreadlocks have emerged, You're still wearing the same jeans from three days ago. And your boot has jewelry, too. You're wearing sparkle pink-glo lip balm, blowing chewing gum bubbles. Celebrate freedom!
WEATHER	Is that a rain cloud? Should I ride in the rain? Is it too windy? Is it too cold?	You find a Zen state in the rain and tame the reflexes. You're tacking the wind like a pro sailing champion, seeing how much gas the bike will actually burn as it fights the headwinds. Electric gear is your friend. You're one with nature!
ATTITUDE	Am I crazy to just get out here like this and ride away from everything I've got to do today?	Sunshine on my shoulders makes me happy! Born to be wild! Free bird! The road is my home! Everyday is a winding road! No quick fix in the world can fine-tune your attitude like a motorcycle ride can!

The Motorcycle becomes an extension of your body. Treat it the way you treat yourself, and your riding time will be that much more enjoyable.

— *Sara Liberte, RT's North Hills Cycle, Inc.; author, journalist, custom bike designer, fine art photographer, and Garage Girl*

Living life caged, all comfy, like when you're riding around in a Lexus, can make you forget about your nature. Are we human beings or human doings? Exposed to nature on a motorcycle we remember, ah, we are ONE with the landscape, the environment, the dogs chasing our bikes, the rain, the sun, the wind. In a car, or worse, a minivan, our thoughts are caged; we're always thinking about gotta do this or that. We're worried or anxious because our minds become boxed by experience. To live out loud in a cage simply means turning up the volume on our stereos. But what if we decide to expose ourselves to something two-wheeled and listen to a new tune in our hearts, take a different route from routine? What if we alter the course of life a little bit by becoming exposed to the elements of living full throttle? What if we are just the two-wheeled Chrome Cowgirl explorer? That's the ultimate motocure, the ultimate fix for mind, body, and soul.

Keeping your motorcycle *motocured* is essential to enjoying the ride. One must not neglect the cries for high maintenance; your chrome horse will whine if you neglect it.

If you follow the T-CLOCS inspection, that's a good reference for generally maintaining your bike. For instance, tire pressure is a neglected little bit of maintenance that is easily correctable but can cause large problems if it isn't. It's like wearing a really awesome pair of shoes with soles that are ripped and heel taps missing. You're going to walk wobbly. Forget about running. That's what it's like when your tire pressure is off. Squirrelly experience. Always refer to your motorcycle owner's manual. That's the cookin' book for answers about your wild ride.

FUEL FOR THOUGHT

Feel the rhythm of the road, deep inside your soul. When you shake off the cacophonous tempo of daily routine and embrace the rhythm of the road, a new song emerges, a melody that makes you shout for joy. You are in tune with the moment, enjoying the harmony of adventure and the symphony up ahead. And so you rock and roll down the road.

When it comes to general maintenance, the motorcycle shop manual for your motorcycle brand and model is full of hearty recipes for keeping the bike in good working order. Maintaining a motorcycle is like cooking or following a recipe. There are ingredients and tools to create a successful outcome. It's a matter of familiarity with the process. Learn the basics of motorcycle maintenance, even if you don't maintain your own ride. Riders like me don't have a whole lot of time to take care of our own bikes. Luckily, I have my Chrome Charming to help me with it, or I take it to a reputable shop.

When you take your bike to a shop, make sure you get references for that motor doctor because, like anything in life, you need to read between the lines and be up on the jive talking. You can ask

The Motorcycle Tool Kit for the Road

- ★ Windzone Tool Kit or CruzTOOLS Kit
- ★ A pack of three red oil rags
- ★ Extra spark plugs
- ★ Extra bulbs
- ★ Quart of oil
- ★ Duct tape
- ★ Electrical tape
- ★ Extra fuses
- ★ Air pressure gauge
- ★ Stop & Go Tire Plugger Kit

- ★ Locks and lock alarm
- ★ Fun bandanas
- ★ First-aid kit
- ★ Earplugs
- ★ Flashlight
- ★ Extra Ziploc baggies
- ★ Pocket road atlas
- ★ Leatherman
- ★ Matches
- ★ Cable ties
- ★ Bungees

- ★ Disposable rubber gloves
- ★ Notebook and paper
- ★ Disposable camera
- ★ Compact umbrella
- ★ Wet Naps
- ★ Motorex Viso-Clean
- ★ Calling card
- ★ Road member cards
- ★ Spare key
- ★ Chrome Cowgirl attitude hat

Tigerlily lined up for an ol' skool checkup before I hit the road to Sturgis (Panhead Phil's Music City Motorcycles).

local motorcycle clubs how to find the local masters of motorcycle repair and maintenance. When you walk into those garages, get that Chrome Cowgirl take-no-bullshit attitude on and smile. Bad ass with pistol-packin' class. And remember to price around . . . just like your inner shopper always loves to do.

DRESS LIKE YOUR INNER CHROME COWGIRL: BE YOURSELF, FIND YOUR COWGIRL

Karen Davidson of the Harley-Davidson Motor Company is the queen of motorcycle fashion. She's got that temperature thing down because you can look both hot and cool wearing those Harley outfits.

TRIP TIP
Make sure you get a motorcycle seat that not only is comfortable, but makes your butt look great.

Slap me five and high my five. The whole idea about being a female rider is being a female rider. Girl. You know, looking like a girl if you're into being feminine. Karen has that locked down. Hailing from the mother ship family in the motorcycle culture, Harley-Davidson, she understands fit, form, function, and fashion all

Tire Burnouts

We're going to learn how to do a tire burnout because you know you want to. Plus, a tire burnout is fun to do anywhere you want to leave your branding mark.

Your used back tire, a.k.a sneaker, is due for a change, so let's have a little fun and give an ode to that ol' back tire that ran you miles around the country:

★ Make sure to brace your front tire up against something stable, or be sure you can hang on to the bike anywhere you burn that back sneaker.

★ Hold the front brake tight.

★ Stand up straight over your seat with both feet planted into the ground.

★ Squeeze the bike a little bit with your knees to keep it from shifting too far to the left or right when that tire is humming full speed (or you can make designs by letting the bike move from side to side while burning rubber).

★ With your motorcycle running, put it into second gear, but, of course, don't release the front brake at all, or the clutch, yet. Keep them pulled in tight.

★ Roll the throttle open with your right thumb and bottom part of your palm, but keep the other right-hand fingers on that brake, and keep that clutch pulled in with your left hand!

★ Slowly release your clutch, but keep that front break tight the whole time, as you open that throttle wide. Keep rockin the throttle.

★ Smoke that tire, baby! Smoke it good!

★ Pull in the clutch and let off the throttle, let off the brake and you're done.

★ Now go get yourself a new back tire.

at once, and she produces and rides the hell out of motorcycles. Lots of other companies have recently followed suit with vivid, bright colors and racy attire. I find that some of the outdoorsy companies also have highly functional gear that can serve as biker chic.

I'm into what I refer to as *road jeans*. I collect all kinds of road treasures on my rides, and then those items that can be glued, stitched, or hitched onto my jeans become a part of the road theme from that trip on those jeans. Other treasures become moto-art and end up as part of a road trip vision on canvas. Mixed media indeed as odd treasures, photos, paint, ink, and scrap supplies merge together onto a pair of yard-sale jeans to become a very artful reflection of my road trip.

I relive the memories of my motorcycle trips whenever I wear my road jeans.

TRIP TIP
Rarely bring dry-clean-only street clothes; they'll only get ruined and smell. Never wear strange fabrics that will melt from exhaust pipe heat. Forget those sexy rubber pants.

And the footwear. Love it. I highly recommend a sexy, gorgeous pair of heeled riding boots. Also, a pair of heeled sandals at the close of a riding day not only cools the feet but looks fabulous and makes you feel oh so versatile and comfortable as a road hag-scooter tramp-Chrome Cowgirl all in one day. Throw on a cute jacket and lipstick, and who even notices that bug splat on the side of your cheek and the road grime pattern upon your neck. For some Chrome Cowboys, well that is the sign of a *keeper*.

I love a sale. In fact, I bowled a dude right down at a Harley-Davidson dealership swap meet for a spoke front wheel. We girls know how to eye it and then seize it. I can pounce like a kitty on a bargain.

There I was, holding a pair of fabulous Harley-Davidson studded wedge sandals in one hand with hats and shirts in another, and I screamed out, "That's mine, that spoke wheel!" I didn't even know if that sum beech would fit! Oh, I pushed a bunch of dudes sweetly to the side as I rushed 'em. I swung my merch over my shoulder and

Only the least amount of baggage will do. Lighten up and ride free! It's all about moving through life with an easy load.

These are the qualities of being: attention, intention, choice, practice, surrender, intuition, gratitude, and trust. Each of these qualities relates in a special way to the divine feminine.

— *Reverend Mary Murray Shelton*

TRIP TIP

Roll your clothes into tight little barrels when you pack, and you'll be able to make room for those road treasures you're bound to purchase. Or, you can just ship stuff back home or to yourself on the road, or just get yourself those vacuum bags and fit everything into a two-inch-tall vacuum-packed bag!

plucked that front wheel right off the display grid. I then dashed off running with the goods to the cash register. And you know, that freakin' spoke wheel does fit!

Gearing up for the ride is power dressing, and you can take that power dressing into your daily life. Wear a shirt proclaiming your visit to a big motorcycle rally beneath your suit jacket. It'll make quite a conversation piece around the office.

Riding is about celebrating. Wearing clothes that reflect your inner joy, coupled with gearing up for the road, creates that unique style that you have in your riding heart. You may want to place a tiara over your bandana-'ed head when you remove your helmet. I keep my tiara handy so that if I stop for a long period of time it's as quick as putting on a cowgirl hat!

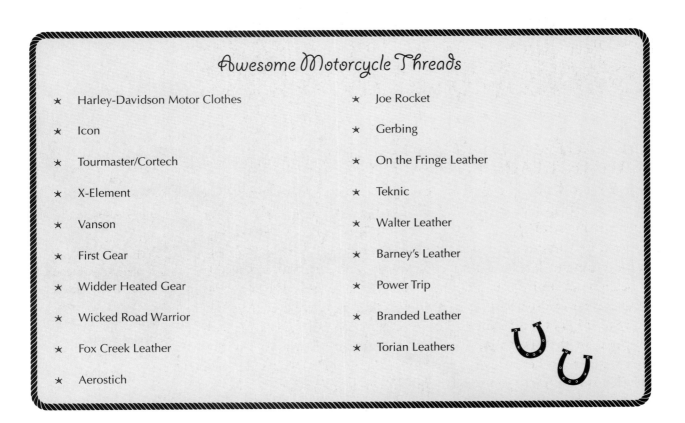

Awesome Motorcycle Threads

- ★ Harley-Davidson Motor Clothes
- ★ Icon
- ★ Tourmaster/Cortech
- ★ X-Element
- ★ Vanson
- ★ First Gear
- ★ Widder Heated Gear
- ★ Wicked Road Warrior
- ★ Fox Creek Leather
- ★ Aerostich

- ★ Joe Rocket
- ★ Gerbing
- ★ On the Fringe Leather
- ★ Teknic
- ★ Walter Leather
- ★ Barney's Leather
- ★ Power Trip
- ★ Branded Leather
- ★ Torian Leathers

Rally ho! Tendin' bar at the Broken Spoke Saloon.
Chris Karash

BAGGAGE MANAGEMENT:
YOU CAN'T PACK TWO PAIRS OF PRADAS!

Lighten the load. That's what you have to do when you ride a motorcycle. You just can't carry all that damn baggage: emotional, physical, or stuff. On a motorcycle there's only room for fun, inspiration, humor, and a small amount of functional riding accessories and equipment! When riding a motorcycle, you quickly learn how to become a minimalist, and a very resourceful one, too. Items have double or triple uses. Lots of things get reused, rewashed, recycled on the road. That chrome horse does not want to be weighed down with baggage. So, the first thing to consider is riding gear, then shoes, and then regular clothes, okay . . . jewelry, makeup, hair thingies . . . but there's a way to manage the baggage. Surrender! Pack light. You just need to be free!

TRIP TIP
You're amazing all the time, even when you have bugs in your teeth and road dirt on your face, but always take a quick check in the mirror for anything glaring like streaked mascara.

My clothing menu BEFORE—based upon a 7-day run

* 4 pairs of jeans
* 2 pairs of funky pants
* 2 pairs of shorts
* 2 pairs of lounging pants
* 3 long-sleeved shirts
* 2 dresses
* 1 miniskirt
* 8 spaghetti-strap tops
* 4 tee shirts

* 1 pair of riding boots
* 1 pair of cowboy boots
* 1 pair of converse sneakers
* 1 pair of sandals
* 1 pair of flip-flops
* 1 lightweight leather jacket
* 1 heavyweight leather jacket
* 1 leather riding shirt
* 2 leather vests

* 1 pair of chaps
* 1 pair of leather riding pants
* 2 purses
* 3 pairs of gloves
* 8 pairs of socks
* 9 pairs of panties
* 4 pairs of sunglasses
* 2 pairs of riding glasses
* 4 attitude hats

My clothing menu AFTER—based upon a 14-day run

* 2 pairs of jeans
* 1 pair of funky pants
* 1 pair of shorts
* 1 pair of lounging pants
* 2 long-sleeved shirts
* 1 thermal shirt
* 1 pair of thermal pants
* 2 tee shirts
* 2 tank tops

* 1 pair of chaps
* 1 pair of leather pants
* 1 leather vest
* 1 leather jacket
* 1 wind-resistant fleece
* 1 leather/fleece neck warmer
* 2 pairs of riding gloves; lightweight and heavyweight
* 1 pair of Dr. Socks warmest grade socks

* 5 pairs of panties
* 5 pairs of socks, assorted
* 1 pair of shower flip-flops
* 1 pair of sexy shoes or sandals
* 1 pair of attractive, functional riding boots
* 1 pair of fun sunglasses
* 2 pairs of riding glasses
* 1 poncho blanket
* Jewelry, including my tiara!

First, if you can afford to, you get all the nice motorcycle baggage like saddlebags, T-bag, tank bag. Or, you do what I do. I have old saddlebags that are taped together with duct tape, and I line those with trash compactor bags and put my things in there. Then I have an old gym bag that I use to carry things that fits really nicely on the back fender and drapes onto the saddlebags so it serves as a nice base to pile a few more things on, pyramid-style: tent, sleeping bag, my hats. Everything is bungee queen'd onto my bike, battened down with several single-strand bungees, layered with net bungees, then topped with single-strand bungees, making the pack virtually

Opposite page: Here are my packing lists. I offer a before-and-after packing list because, just like everyone who starts out riding, I packed way too much and ended up shipping stuff back home from the road.

My cool tiara, purchased at Lynn's Dakota Mart, Lazelle Street, Sturgis, South Dakota. *Michele Lanci-Altomare*

TRIP TIP
Never wear false eyelashes when you ride over 25 miles per hour. They will end up looking like dead caterpillars on your eyelids.

HAIRDO BY HELMET

immovable. I pride myself on my ragamuffin bungee abilities. In fact, bungees come in very handy for other things, such as a belt to keep the wind from puffing up your coat, as a clamp around your ankles to keep your pants from blowing up your knees, as a bracelet to keep the air out from between your gloves and sleeve opening. I've also bungeed my windshield to my bike when it snapped off in a rain and windstorm. I also used duct tape to secure it. That stayed that way for a little over a year until I could finally get a new clamp for it. I tied a bandana around the bungee–duct tape Band-Aid I created, and it really made my bike look very road veteran.

Motorcycle Madamoiselle's Beauty Kit for the Road

* Body Shop body spray

* Max Factor Lash Perfection waterproof mascara

* Eyelash curler

* Oil of Olay daily facial wipes

* Neutrogena Ultra Sheer, Dry-Touch Sunblock SPF 70

* Listerine vanilla mint mouthwash

* Bobbi Brown bronzing powder

* Stila eye shadow stick

* Kiehl's lip balm SPF 15 in a pretty hue for day-long riding

* Kiehl's Pink Rider lip gloss

* Nail file

* A pair of Harley-Davidson heeled sandals

* Creative Scentsations Vanilla Shimmer Hand & Body Lotion

* Spring Fresh organic deodorant

* Purel

* Tiara

Note: Keep most of these beauty treats really handy for quick roadside touch-ups.

A smelly hippie from road funk, but at least I'm wearing a skirt and tiara.

My bike and I are a team; if one fails, we both fail.

— *Valerie Iengo, a.k.a. Road Warrior*

TRIP TIP
Make sure you get a motorcycle seat that not only is comfortable, but it makes your butt look great.

Brother Speed is a master Roadini and has been a wise guy to this Chrome Cowgirl over the years.

Life is good and so is the journey!

— Pepper S. Massey,
Director, Sturgis Rally Department

Route 5
ROADINI
Road Magic and Tips & Tricks

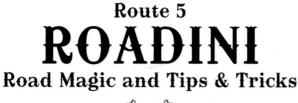

You need to be a *Roadini* if you ride a motorcycle. That means you have to work your magic, girl, to make some things happen when all other solutions seem impossible. Be prepared to use your arts and crafts instinct and that wonderful can-do-anything-you-put-your-mind-to attitude. You'll encounter some challenging things on a motorcycle journey out there in wild wanderlust wonderland.

Riding is a nature- and soul-oriented activity because as you ride through landscape filled with wild wonder, your soul is engaged in the moment of wanderlust, and at the same time you ponder ideas that are far reaching yet fantastically possible. To be seated in that forward-moving, two-wheeled place while all seems still and serene is a heavenly place to be, one that we love to share with our riding sisters and brothers.

Here's a quick twenty-minute workout:

* ★ Jump rope one minute.
* ★ Do a twelve-rep set of tube workouts: one set of biceps, one set of triceps, one set of shoulders.
* ★ Jump rope one minute.
* ★ Do another round of muscle sets.
* ★ Jump rope two minutes.
* ★ Do a final round of sets.
* ★ Do a vigorous thirty-second jump rope.
* ★ Perform one set of lunges, one set of squats, and fifty crunches.

Stretch a bit, and now you're done. Twenty minutes. You're ready to ride.

Refueling with corn—the body's biodiesel.

How to Transform Road Food

TAKE THAT FATTENING MENU AND TRANSFORM IT INTO DELICIOUS SKINNY FARE!

BEFORE—FAST FOOD	AFTER—FIT FOOD
cheeseburger, French fries, and a Coke	burger (no bun), cottage cheese on lettuce, sliced tomatoes and onions, and water with lots of lemon
fried eggs, bacon, and white toast	two poached eggs with sliced tomatoes, one slice of whole wheat toast, and everything drizzled with virgin olive oil and sprinkled with salt, pepper, and parmesan cheese
potato chips, Doodles, tortilla chips	carrot sticks, celery, apples, grapes, and oranges, kashi bars
beer	beer
soda	water with peppermint oil

Food Kit

organic raw food bars	EmergenC energy powder
powder meal replacements	almonds
vitamins: omegas, multivitamin, vitamin B	water bottle

The Wheel is a deep-structure portrait of nature-and-soul-oriented cultures, a portrait that encompasses child-raising practices, core values, stages of growth, rites of passage, community organization, and relationship to the greater earth community.

— *Bill Plotkin,* Nature and the Human Soul

WHEN PEEING AT THE GAS STATION BATHROOM IS NOT AN OPTION: HOW TO BE REALLY RESOURCEFUL

As a Chrome Cowgirl pioneering the open roads, be prepared because you're gonna get dirty and wet, and you're gonna have a lot of fun. Memories made on a motorcycle journey never get old; they always stay accessible and give you a fresh injection of energy from reliving an amazing experience. There are a lot of things that happen on the road that differ from anything you're used to, which makes it such a thrill . . . and sometimes not so thrilling.

Like peeing at a gas station. Why wouldn't it be a good option? Well, if you're all stuffed into some rain gear and you enter that filthy bathroom, you'll realize that you'd rather hold it because I guarantee you're going to have to fight that rain gear off of you, you're going to stumble, and your ass is going to hit that seat. I don't care how much squatting strength you have. Also, it's really hard to roll up the pants and the rain gear so your garments aren't hanging on the urine-covered floor.

I suggest stopping at a fantastic-looking hotel. A female motorcycle rider is rarely, if ever, denied the opportunity to pee in fancy rest facilities no matter how grimy she is after riding in bad weather. Ah, the vision of waltzing dirty and wet into a hotel lobby and into the bathroom, only to encounter a lovely bride in white. . . . You'll feel more like a queen for the day than she does.

TRIP TIP
A pair of red panties can cover over a cracked taillight in a pinch.

READING ROAD SIGNS AND INNER MAPS: INTUITIVE MAPQUESTING

We all know how to read road signs—"No Left Turn," "Yield to Oncoming Traffic," "Do Not Enter"—but out on the road we need to learn to read less obvious signs, the subtle directions we get from nature, our bodies, and our bikes. A Chrome Cowgirl often lets instinct drive her, using these less obvious signs for guidance.

Motorcycle ESP

Extrasensory perception is normally associated with mental activities like telepathy, clairvoyance, and precognition. As riders, we might feel that sometimes our ESP kicks in, enabling us to do the right thing to avoid a collision or bad riding situation. One psychology major who designed an ESP experiment linked ESP to a relaxed state of mind and a freer level of consciousness. For me, this is where motorcycling really enters the picture. As far as I'm concerned, riding promotes a more relaxed state of mind and puts me on a higher level of consciousness than where I usually am.

— Amy Holland, publisher and editor, *Friction Zone* magazine

P.S. Did you know that there is another kind of motorcycle ESP? And that's when your whole life revolves around Exciting Saddle Priority.

Nature's signs are often the most dramatic, and you ignore them at your own peril.

Unless you're a farmer or meteorologist, you may not have acquired the skill needed to read the skies. Some riders start putting on that rain gear as soon as they see a cloud. I like to wait until I can smell the rain. If it looks like a storm is up ahead, I check out the windshields in the opposite lane to see if there are any wipers moving.

There are times when I don't put on any rain gear, especially when it's really hot outside because to me it feels awesome to get wet after being completely hot. You may not feel the same. You may be more susceptible to colds and all that. But I've had some fun moments riding drenched in a rainstorm after the temperatures had reached one hundred degrees. On the other hand, there's nothing more chilling than getting hit with a rainstorm while you're riding in cooler weather. The temperature drops quickly when it rains; sometimes it gets so cold that your nipples could cut glass.

HOW TO PICK UP A DROPPED BIKE

Every once in a while the unexpected happens. When the unexpected happens on a motorcycle, one of the possible consequences is that your motorcycle will fall over. Don't worry; it happens to everyone. Here are your options for righting your beloved motorcycle when she keels over:

★ Option A: Chill out, turn off the engine, turn off the gas if you can reach it, kiss the tank, and remove any loose luggage that may have fallen. Then put the downed steed into gear if you can, get the kickstand down as soon as possible, bend your knees, butt against the seat, grab that grip closest to the ground and turn the handlebars toward the tank so the wheel's pointing toward the ground. Hang on to that grip tight, then with your other hand grab something secure like the fender or saddlebag rails, bend deep in the knees with your butt square in the middle of the seat, and take baby steps backward, pressing your butt into the seat as you walk the bike upright while pushing into it. (Hey, boys, watch this!)

TRIP TIP
Ward off wrinkles!
Ward off road fatigue!
Keep hydrated.
Drink water at every stop, even if you're not thirsty.

Road Diary:

Not far up the road, I met a highway hero. Steve was his name. A bunch of us were piled up at a gas station shaking off the road willies from having to concentrate so hard trying to see through the heavy fog that came down like a fallen cloud. "Hey, we saw you pass us by," a couple of boys said. "Cool ride."

"Thank you. She likes to go fast even when she should be tame," I explained about Miss Tigerlily. They thought I was talking about myself. Well, I was, in effect, because Tigerlily is an extension of my soul.

I checked Miss Tigerlily's oil and she was low. Crap. I should have gotten a quart when I was at that Pilot gas station in Murdo. Whatever. I'd flag a chrome friend down and see if they had any because this tiny gas station in the middle of the prairie didn't have what I needed.

There was Steve, a handsome fellow, strong, silent type. I did the whole, "Hey, honey, can you spot me some oil? I'll pay ya." He was on it like lightning. He even rode his bike over to where Miss Tigerlily was just shakin' her stuff. What a flirt my bike is . . . he gave me the quart. I only needed half. He insisted on me keeping the quart . . . but I gave it back.

We were road kin from that moment on. That's what I love about the road; it is a kinship. You so care and love that other rider because you know . . . you secretly know . . . you are vibin' with the glorious mystique of being road warriors, taking on the adventure, ditching routine, riding away from what everybody else expects, and going deep into the camaraderie and the transformation that happens to you out here . . . as lone rangers or riding pack wild in a club.

I took off and headed to the Badlands, and wouldn't you know it, there again I would run into the Highway Hero Steve and his road brothers. So, our bikes danced and skipped together through the Badlands for a spell, until Tigerlily just wanted to be her little classy bad-ass soulo self, winding through the canyons. Farewell, highway hero. You sure were a nice vision of motor-oil-bearing eye candy.

Groan a lot like a road warrior. Now you can see why engine guards are awesome because they cradle your ride when it tips over so that it's easier to push back up.

★ Option B: Turn off the engine, turn off the gas if you can reach it, kiss the tank, and remove any luggage that may have gone astray in the fall. Then take a red oil rag and yoo-hoo it in the air at passing vehicles.

★ Option C: Turn off the engine, turn off the gas if you can reach it, remove any luggage that may have gone astray in the fall, smile in a feline way at the boys, and get your girl-power buddies to help you. Then high-five one another and be on your way.

FUEL FOR THOUGHT

Salad bars and organic food bars are a girl's best friend. Healthy eating on the road contributes to your inner glow and fuels your girl power. Water wards off wind wrinkles and reduces bloating. Fried foods, sugar, and excessive starches give a Chrome Cowgirl PMS (parked motorcycle syndrome), making her sluggish and cranky. When you tour on a motorcycle, your most important responsibility is to maintain your body. If you neglect your body, there's not a lot you can do when you get sick in the middle of some empty desert.

This is love. This is life on the road. The Christian Motorcycle Association cleans your windshields and provides fresh water, all for the love of their fellow riders and Jesus.

THE ROAD OF OPPORTUNITY

Once you embark upon a journey and you're far from your normal routine, your whole world opens up like in *Alice in Wonderland*. Stories come to you, and you become a part of other people's stories. Folks will see a vision of liberty gloriously astride her chrome horse, and you will become exciting dinner talk for them that evening. Others will see you as a biker bitch ready to take over the town, and thus you become the hot gossip at bingo for the week.

Charles Kuralt is my journalism hero because he was a road junkie. Even though he tooled around the countryside in an RV and not on two wheels, he was all about getting deep into exploring the road and the surprises it offers. He knew the stories that come from the road from just being out there. I've learned that "the road,"

I was used to going fast and working hard. "On The Road" seemed to work best when I went slow and took it easy. I found that while it helped to have a story in mind up the road somewhere, the world would not come to an end if I never got there; I might find something more interesting along the way. It was best to take a deep breath, mosey along and soak up the moods of the country and the changes of weather and terrain. When I finally shook off the tempo of daily journalism and fell in to the rhythms of the country-side, I didn't have to worry about finding stories any longer. They found me.

— *Charles Kuralt, author and CBS news anchor, Sunday morning*
On the Road with Charles Kuralt

Life in suspension, swinging forward in full swing. On a motorcycle it's all about swinging forward; the demands of life as you know it suspend for a while. *Jodi Ray Sorensen*

FUEL FOR THOUGHT

Attitude Check Time—Do You Have Your Rev On? Nothing is more of a downer out there on the open road than being tired and grumpy. The main reason we get tired and grumpy on a ride is because we don't eat right or take care of our sexy selves. Nothing gives us the kind of downer that's caused by not taking care of ourselves on our motorcycle journey. We've got to realize that just as our bikes require premium fuel to run at top notch, so do our bodies. Our greatest resource out there on the road is our strongest self—body, mind, and soul—so that we can have a powerful and engaging experience while riding our motorcycles.

especially experiencing it on a motorcycle, produces stories that truly are beyond imagination. Oftentimes these experiences are so very humbling that you genuinely feel the power of what it means to be one with something—the moment sinks you into the definition of living. Charles Kuralt found those stories and those stories found him because he was open to whatever may happen. That's living in the moment—the edge of anticipation, when we open our souls up like magnets to attract the depths of adventure. That magic happens when we free our minds from the gravity of thought and we're not caught up in the past or future. Instead, we just welcome the new weightless experiences of the present moment.

Opportunity finds you on the open road. Be prepared to course-correct your life because your two-wheeled freedom machine will turn on lots of light bulbs in your head. Maybe that's why, in order to make our dreams come true, we have to embark upon a journey to discover those dreams. You figure things out while you're out there, lost in motorcycle meandering. If a dream were easy to achieve there would be no reason to go searching for it. Often I think that dreams want to be chased, the way a child wants to play a game of catch me if you can. That's a good allegory for the playful moment that

Life is a canyon of opportunity. Riding is all about living on the edge of opportunity, a vast and wide canyon of hopes and dreams to behold.

Things to do if you run out of fuel in the middle of nowhere

★ Pray that you'll get some fuel somewhere, anywhere!

★ Flag down a trailer queen with a fancy motorcycle in tow. They always have gas because they don't ride that much.

★ Siphon gas out of a nice car. Keep a siphoning kit handy.

★ Keep spare gas! Carry it in one of those small MX gas cans.

★ Never leave your bike. Convince a kind motorist to go get you some gas and bring it back to you.

The "Garage Girls" are wrench-wielding duo Sara Liberte and Jody Perewitz, windsisters who prove girls love their garages, too. *Sara Liberte*

bubbles up inside of the motorcycle rider because our bikes take us back to a certain innocence, an innocence that comes from admitting we don't really know what will happen on this journey. But on our bikes we don't really think about such unimportant matters; we are seated in wild wonder listening to our inner Cheshire Cat with a glowing grin.

WRENCHING AND RIDING

As a Chrome Cowgirl, you'll encounter all kinds of firsts (part of the fun is learning to cope with it all), and sooner or later you will have to learn to cope with a breakdown. How to deal with breakdowns is something riders learn on the fly. Many people who ride don't work on their bikes. Even if you have all the motorcycle mechanic books and DVDs, that valuable info often just sits on the shelves. I highly advise learning a bit about the mechanics of a bike. Not much . . . just watch a basic training DVD. There are all kinds of breakdowns that might happen. For instance, your headlight might go out at night while you're going 65 miles per hour down a dark highway. Yes, this happened to me. I thought perhaps I'd blown a fuse; nope, wasn't a

FUEL FOR THOUGHT

Re-creation = recreation . . . so let's have fun re-creating ourselves. I have this thing about deep breathing. I need to practice reaching deep for my breath on a daily basis so that when I'm physically stationary for any reason, I know that I can access that very deep breath and hyper-energize my body. To work out on the road, carry a jump rope for cardio and an exercise tube to work out your muscles.

YOU CAN LOOK BOTH COOL AND HOT ON A MOTORCYCLE. SMOT

fuse. Maybe the switches in the housing? Wha??? That's a bigger job than I know how to deal with, even in my imagination. So, what to do? Well, let's look at the guts of the light, I decided. So I took apart the light, and lo and behold the wire to the bulb was corroded. I had electrical tape and gadgets to fix it, but how am I supposed to fix it? The Krispy Kreme delivery guy gassing up at the station helped me. So now I know how to fix a corroded wire.

Life is a long ride. It makes no sense to ride it unprepared. How do we prepare for all the twists and turns and things that cross our paths unexpectedly? Apply long-wearing lipstick, keep your pocket humor handy, and pray for prodigious wisdom to greet the sunrise of opportunity and meet the sunset of the unknown before you even set foot out of the house.

One of the biggest drags on a road trip is running out of gas, which happens more than you might think because, since you're having such a good time out there, you forget to turn the bike from reserve to on. Now the reserve and regular tank are both dry. Or you're in the middle of nowhere, where the only gas stations are out of business, and now so is your motorcycle. On those ol' lonesome highways stranded on the side of the road there are some great Samaritans.

No matter how well prepared you are, no matter how skilled a rider or mechanic, no matter how meticulously maintained your motorcycle, no matter how lucky you are, eventually you will run into a problem that is beyond your power to fix. It doesn't matter if

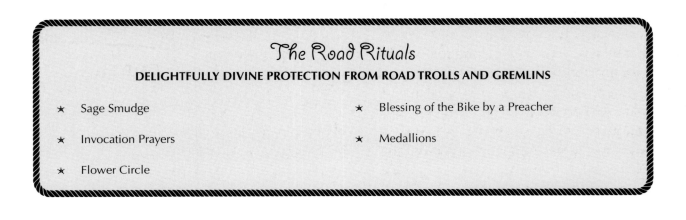

The Road Rituals
DELIGHTFULLY DIVINE PROTECTION FROM ROAD TROLLS AND GREMLINS

- ★ Sage Smudge
- ★ Invocation Prayers
- ★ Flower Circle
- ★ Blessing of the Bike by a Preacher
- ★ Medallions

you are the sort of resourceful character who can make a small-scale nuclear device from a tampon applicator and a paper clip, you will eventually run into a problem that you cannot solve by yourself.

At times like this, you might as well pray. If, like me, you believe in the power of prayer, this might actually help get you out of a jam. You might as well pray even if you are a dogmatic atheist because when you reach such an impasse, at the very least prayer won't make the situation any worse.

EXAMPLES OF ROADSIDE PRAYERS: DEAR GOD . . .

* Thank you for saving me from a stale life.
* Please transmit some knowledge into my brain so that I can figure out why my bike won't start!
* I'm lost. Please find me.
* Please get me to the next gas station. I promise I won't cuss again.
* You were right. This is living. I'll never be a prisoner to a job I hate ever again.

ROAD ANGELS

One thing about riding is this: who gives a crap what anybody thinks about you? Thoughts from others are colored by their own life experiences. Judgments others make have no validity. We live by the way of our truth and let the big spirit express our hearts. The trip belongs to you and that bike you're saddled on, be it a Harley or an old Honda. Life on a motorcycle belongs to your very unique personality; it all belongs to *you* as *you* see fit. Nobody else is riding that bike you're on and taking that road as you ride it. You make your own tips and tricks out there that suit your fancy. You dress however you want and be the person you love to be. Don't ever give into bike shame. Don't feel guilty about not having a fancy bike, and don't ever give in to how-you-dress shame because you're not wearing the latest and greatest, fancy, name-brand road gear. Riding is truth. Ride whatever you want to ride if it makes you happy. Motorcycle riding is about having fun.

TRIP TIP
Here's a fun cheatie campfire snack: Fritos corn chips and sugar Corn Pops mixed together.

This is a position that I assume regularly before and after I ride. *Jason Marshall*

Never be afraid to embark upon a road trip. Just think of it as a *Wizard of Oz*–style adventure and be prepared as best you can. Sadly, I've run into lots of riders who are timid about going on a road trip solo. While it's fun to ride with a group of buddies, riding solo has far-reaching merits that fan the fires burning in your soul into a full-blaze road-tripping adventure filled with high concept storylines that not even the finest writers in Hollywood could conjure up. You'll run into rain, you'll run into bike mechanical failures, heck you may run into a lack of money to even get where you were hoping to go—but out there on the open road, there are road angels, and for some reason, the universe just opens up and connects you to resources even if it seems impossible. The road is a perfect place to exercise the law of attraction because if you free your mind from the past and the what-if angst of the future, then you're in the moment. That's when you'll receive direction and the bright light of awareness. Plan ahead if you want, but stay in the ridelicious moment at all times. Just like a road atlas, there's a map that is drawn on your journey, if you're open to the magic of the road that connects you to people, circumstances, and moments. This map is being charted out of your present moments, and your entire being vibrates from the overwhelming experience. A motorcycle journey positively changes you.

The wheels can't possibly be touching the ground. I feel like I'm flying on my motorcycle through the Badlands, South Dakota. *Michael Lichter*

TRIP TIP
Carry a pretty little umbrella in your saddlebag so that you can catch some shade when you stop during the soaring temperatures, or protect yourself from golf-ball-size hail and pelting rain if there's no shelter!

115

Road Diary:

Badlands Trading Post is the place to find fun road trinkets to decorate your handlebars. I got a little painted arrow, a colorful beaded necklace, and a copper Kokopelli bracelet that I strapped onto the chrome reigns (handlebars) with bread ties and plastic purple cable ties. I am spinning through the Badlands, the land that the great American Indian culture had to endure and respect as the ultimate test of survival.

That makes me think of the television show "Survivor" and their rather protected circumstances compared to the harsh yesterdays endured by these amazing pioneers. Badlands is about the mystery of life. Rugged, jagged, hard, and mean terrain, and then smooth, soft, delicate prairie—a land of extremes. Here I am riding through it and it is extremely hot, dude.

Sunsets are my favorite time here in the Badlands. Sometimes sunrises can be really cold when you climb out of your tent in the morning to greet the majestic spires that let you know the Badlands are bad, baby, bad. When you experience this territory on a motorcycle, I recommend camping overnight out here. Go hiking early in the morning. Really dig into this territory and know what your two wheels are spinning upon. This land ain't no foolin'—this represents honest, hard pioneering. And just beyond these tourist lands lay a truth: The Lakota Sioux reservation, Pine Ridge.

The Badlands belong to those who experience and respect the heart of this land. This is where hearts have been broken and restored. My heart is restored from this ride. The ride has connected me to the experience of one wild road trip that just sets my soul soaring with hawks above me. I can't really explain it yet, but I've discovered this interesting concept of acceptance through keeping my mind as in the moment as possible, welcoming each mile with an enthusiastic innocence even though I may have cruised these roads before. No matter how many times you journey the same roads, for instance to Sturgis, it is transforming. The roads might stay the same, but you are different each time. You let go of a lot more in order to let in the moments. Next stop is Sturgis, and I'm meeting up with my beloved windsisters Betsy Huelskamp and Gevin Fax, two Chrome Cowgirl terrors who ride wild and free, dressed like femme fatales—"We're road hags," as Betsy likes to say.

Note how Tigerlily sort of vibrated off a "limb" during the ride from Chamberlain to Badlands. A whole highway arm and peg vanished in the fog! Guess I'll remember to use Loctite next time, eh?

UNCAMPY CAMPING: GETTING THROUGH THE HARD TIMES

To camp on a motorcycle trip is to really get out there and bond with the environment that you ride through. It's work, though. Unpacking that bike and then deciding on how to make all your gear fit inside of your canvas abode, especially if it's a grocery-sack-sized tent made for one person, can scramble the mind. I've finagled all kinds of odd sleeping arrangements in my quest for snoozing in the outdoors. If I have too tiny a tent, I create a tarp canopy that links bike to tent so that I can get a little more room but I can't move inside the tent. . . . I'm cocooned.

TRIP TIP

Wear white long-sleeved shirts when you ride in the summer so that you don't get all hot and bothered. You'll look like a biker angel!

Eventually, I graduated to a bigger tent with all the pop-up quick-setup conveniences, which I highly recommend. Then you can stash all your crap in it and make room for some honey company if you'd like. You can even sit up in a bigger tent and create an *I Dream of Jeannie* sort of interior with all your stuff. I like to carry a lightweight decorative cotton throw made in India. Very versatile. It can be a fancy tablecloth, a nice bedspread, a wrap skirt, or a head scarf. It can be a room divider if you need to share your tent and you want your own space, or it can be a picnic cloth. You can use it as a body wrap with flip-flops when you use the community shower house.

You Know You're a Motorcyclust When

- ★ You kiss your bike good night.

- ★ You kiss your bike good morning.

- ★ You wander out to the garage to mull over life issues and relationship problems with your bike.

- ★ You wash and polish your bike as if you were bathing your lover.

- ★ You'd rather sleep on your bike than leave her alone in a motel parking lot overnight.

- ★ You chain yourself to your bike while you sleep in your tent.

- ★ You use the Internet to plan motorcycle trips while at work.

- ★ You hole up in the corner of your favorite bookstore and pore over the motorcycle magazines.

- ★ Your motorcycle mama instinct is piqued at all times, letting you know if anyone is messing with your motorcycle.

- ★ You decorate your workspace with your wild motorcycle photos, therefore earning you a classy bad-ass title and lots of free lunches with wannabes.

- ★ You carry a wallet-size photo of your bike along with your family photos.

- ★ You cancel a date with a cute guy so that you can go riding.

- ★ You keep a pocket road atlas in your purse and peruse it during latté breaks.

- ★ You get extreme PMS syndrome when you're unable to go to a rally due to inconveniences like work and lack of money.

Jewel of the Asphalt

En route
to Harley-
Davidson's 100th
Anniversary.
*Road-inspired art
by Sasha*

* Your iPod is chock full of motorcycle tunes to get your inner motor revvin'.

* You call your friends and ask how their bikes are doing.

* You wear your biker clothing as regular street wear.

* You paint your nails and toenails the same color as your bike.

* You won't date a guy unless he rides.

* You ditch paying a utility bill so that you can go to the Easyriders Rodeo or to a racing event for the weekend.

* You decide to put your stuff in storage and live on your motorcycle.

* You laugh at events that would normally be highly aggravating had you been in the regular world experiencing such an event.

* You sell your engagement ring and use the dough as a down payment on a motorcycle.

* You can name the motorcycle by the sound of its pipes.

* You stop all conversation and activity when you hear a motorcycle approaching.

* You love to ride tank to tank, visiting the gas station only when dangerously low on fuel.

* You love to tango with your motorcycle in the twists and turns.

* You live for the rush of the wind ripping through your soul while riding.

* You find your motorcycle-riding image quite majestic in the reflection of store windows and mirrored on the sides of tractor trailers.

For a 100 miles-per-hour quick repair, use purple duct tape.
Michele Lanci-Altomare

Outdoorsy Kit

★ Tent—a sturdy, quick-setup kind

★ Self-inflating sleeping mat

★ Off bug repellent

★ Tarp

★ LED headlamp

★ Incense

★ Chimes

★ Use your Twister mat for the tent floor, too

I'd rather sleep under a zillion stars instead of staying in a five-star hotel.

Lighting incense around the fire can create a sensual mood. Sometimes I'll burn a few sticks at once, stick them in the ground, and watch the smoke swirl in with the campfire. It's a tantalizing scent indeed, with the music of nature floating around you.

A comfy room down the street at a hotel is fine, with all the conveniences, a TV and personal bathroom and all—but it sort of removes you from the organic feel of pioneering. The experience of camping under the stars with the fireflies flashing in the deep darkness creates a magical moment. Let your skin feel the dampness as night creeps in and the temperature drops, stirring something wild inside of you.

The magic of an evening spent outdoors enhances my experience of riding through nature during the day. Air conditioning becomes

TRIP TIP

Join premium plus AAA! They have all kinds of great services and discounts, as does the American Motorcyclist Association. You can join motorcycle manufacturer member clubs, too, for some rockin' ridin' deals.

> **So we speak, not as pleasing men,**
> **but God who examines our hearts.**
>
> *— 1 Thessalonians 2:4*

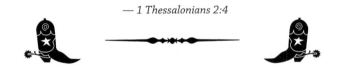

I also taught my cat GypZ Jingles how to go camping in her own tent. I only wish she'd learn to love to ride with me, too!

something artificial. I sweat and burn on the ride. Sometimes I freeze in the cold, damp weather. Other times the weather is gentle and perfect. No matter what, I crave camping. Camping is wild. It is abandoning life as you know it with all its creature comforts. Comfort takes on a whole new meaning out there on the open road. You expose yourself, racing down the highway, experiencing the ecstasy of speed, perhaps racing the storm cloud coming in, or riding into the sunset, making more mileage that day than anticipated. Reservations at campgrounds are great, but sometimes you're not quite sure where you may land if you're not on the clock and you're letting your inner mileage craving govern the ride.

It's true that chopper gypsies, scooter tramps, and mileage thieves hang out at amazing campgrounds. There are all kinds of folks to meet at a campground, and next thing you know you're all sitting around the campfire jawing and laughing.

Now, of course, there are times when one must trailer due to physical limitations. But there are a lot of folks out there who just like to ride around the rally disrespecting other riders with their egotistic riding mannerisms. They simply do not respect the culture, nor do they understand the concept of the journey when you try to explain.

TRIP TIP
Remember that on an adventure, safety comes first in every move we make. Wisdom = Safety.

You know these chrome horses are just dying to run the asphalt prairie through which they travel imprisoned in the back of a truck.

Three top tips for beating a moving violation (with a male officer)

★ Shift around on your seat and say, "Officer, I've got to pee."

★ Smile and purse your lips like the chicks in the motorcycle calendars and say, "Well, you look like you're a rider, too."

★ Remove your helmet and toss your hair around while you rummage for your identification, and then say, "I was lost in the moment of the ride. Pardon me while I undress to find my information."

These cowboys were impressed that I travel all over the country on my little Harley.

TRIP TIP

Use a Twister mat to protect your stuff from the weather. Net bungee it over the tail pack. It's visible in the rain, and you can use it for some roadside fun.

TRUCK STOP SHOPPIN': KITSCHY TREASURES FOR THE JOURNEY OF LIFE

I've found many treasures at truck stops. My road jeans will attest to that. How many coffees have I vacuumed into my shivering little body? Too many to count. I've spent nights in truck stops . . . not as a lot lizard, no, but as this worn-out chick on a motorcycle with no place to lay my sleepy head. Sometimes I've spent the night in truck stops because I can't sleep and I'm wired to ride, but the road is crawling with the unpredictable moves of wildlife. One time I just didn't have the money to spend anywhere, and I had no tent. That was when I realized I always have to bring my tent with me. So I do.

Once I slept on my bike in the woods behind the Comfort Inn during the day. I just couldn't make it a mile more . . . my eyes were sleepy. Some of us riders are fools for the road. We just love to be out there. We live for the next adventure. It's a high. Pulling up to a

TRIP TIP

Fishing gear makes an excellent windbreaker anytime you need an extra layer. Though a nerdy getup, a rain slicker keeps you warm and dry.

truck stop, or saloon for that matter, and tying up the steed (parking the bike) is a really empowering moment as you saunter into the establishment. All eyes are on the Chrome Cowgirl. Sassy you in dark glasses and your own personal Chrome Cowgirl swagger.

I love that feeling of swaggering into a truck stop in all my riding gear and striking up a conversation with another road hog on a motorcycle. I meet the most interesting folks at truck stops. It's really a unique social event that rapidly changes minute by minute as more travelers stop off for rest, food, fuel, and conversation.

Road-inspired napkin art by Sasha.

There have been moments where I spent nearly all night in a truck stop due to severe weather, and so I wrote in my journal at a lone table with a never-ending cup of coffee. I write fiction about all the characters I see in the place and then invent stories about each one. Napkin art is another favorite truck stop activity. I'll draw little characters of the folks, and sometimes that evolves into cartoon art. I'm not all that good at it, but it's so much fun. Then I'll find some of this art crumbled in a napkin several months later as I reach for an available something in which to blow my nose. And there, at the last minute, I will see the little piece of truck stop art on a stray napkin, while I catch a snottie.

OFF THE BEATEN PATH:
THAT WORLD BETWEEN POINT A AND POINT B

The looser you make your trip, the better the experience will be. Your stories will become tales you couldn't make up if you tried. Offbeat paths are the coolest ways to throw yourself into the great unknown.

Someday I'd like to travel around the country without a map entirely . . . just head off in whichever direction my intuition told me to go, visit those places that are nearly forgotten, or those places where time has stood still and technology is not the priority. That world between A and B, the world between where you set off to and where you're fixin' to go, is where all the exciting things really happen. For instance, a trip to Sturgis could have you on all kinds of back roads that'll carve out the most exciting tour of our country, and the things you will see and experience will get you so hooked on journeying to these rallies, trailering will be a cuss word.

You can be any character you want to be out on the road, whether off the beaten path or galloping down the highway. Like I always say, it's your story, so fill it up with great memories, hysterical tales, contemplative moments, and soul-stirring encounters. Let humor be your constant companion. When you're getting a little too serious and wrapped up in your own stuff, that bit of humor, sometimes in tandem with humility, will rear up and save you from yourself.

TRIP TIP

For a really unpredictable and timeless adventure, take back roads only and follow no map or clock. Stop at only small mom-and-pop operations, honky-tonks, and dives, and visit odd roadside attractions. And remember, detours are side roads begging to be explored.

TRIP TIP

For a fast warm-up at a truck stop, mix half a cup of coffee with a shot of every flavor from the flavored cappuccino machine. What a buzz.

Racing around the track on a chrome horse is like riding a high-speed merry-go-round. *Dennis Curnette*

Live your own dream and follow your heart!

— *Valerie Thompson, Team Owner,*
ValerieThompsonRacing.com

FASTASTIC WINDSISTERS
Twists & Turns

WINDSISTERS:
RIDERS R A GIRLZ BEST FRIEND

What's the definition of a real friend? A sister. A wind-sister. She's there for you, steady as a rock. A windsister understands the importance of keeping relationships strong and keeps your secrets deep in the engine cases of her heart. She'll take every high noon moment you dish at her, and respect you for it. She'll give you a high noon moment so real you'll want to bitch smack yourself for a wake-up call in life.

Back up or get the back up! Windsisters are your best friends for the journey of life.

curves ahead

Chrome Cowgirl Betsy Huelskamp is a windsister to me. She's a fitness instructor and nutritionist and believes in the power of maintaining a fit motorcycle and a fit body to go the distance. *Courtesy of Betsy Huelskamp*

Meeting women mechanics from all around the country while riding solo on my motorcycle has been incredible—a life-changing and wonderfully fulfilling project! The mechanics I have met are very inspiring to me, and I hope that the work I do will inspire other people to follow their dreams as well.

— *Sarah Lyon, creator of the Female*
Mechanics Calendar Project

Gevin is a spiritual windsister native to the American Indians of South Dakota. She's all about road rituals for everyday life.

THE BOND OF WINDSISTERS

How do windsisters bond? We love to group ride in a power pack, in a staggered formation so we have our space to groove down the road. Windsisters love to have a good time, and we are experts at seeking out those good times and attracting them. We love disco dancing in chaps and watching our fringe spin free in the techno lights; dancing on honky tonk bars Hogs-&-Heifers style; those late-night tipsy fireside chats; riding mechanical bulls two at a time; and no matter what we're doing, we command attention everywhere and anywhere we go. Why is that? Because we are the picture of liberty, freedom, and *Girls Just Want to Have Fun.* Like a most cherished secret, we love to share our passion for riding with one another. Soul expansion happens when you're out there together roaming the countryside,

We spend a great deal of time I think, thinking about time. It occurred to me that there are days I look in the mirror and don't recognize myself. I'm actually startled that I'm older. Imagine! It's not that I've lost track and don't remember how old I am; it's that inside I don't feel that way. Inside I feel the same way I did when I was a ridiculously silly teenager.

I hope I never grow up. Having said that, I'm so much better today than I was back then and wouldn't trade the happiness and tears, the experiences that ripped me up and molded me, the abundance of love and happiness I've known, for anything.

Life is good and so is the journey!

— *Pepper S. Massey, Director, Sturgis Rally Department*

TRIP TIP

For a better pack-wild group riding experience, ride in staggered formation so that you have your own space and passersby can see how cool your bike is.

Road Diary:

There's something about sleeping on the ground that puts me in a grounded mood. Priorities straighten out when you lie there listening to the night music of crickets and the early morning bird songs. I'm tucked in a canvas den and the dew on the tent drips in spots right onto my face. Gosh, that's a lot of cleaning God has to do in the night. Like a soul janitor scrubbing our insides out and our minds clean and fresh so that he can talk to us and maybe, if we have removed ourselves from all the distractions, we can listen.

We move through the transition time between evening and dawn when the moon governs the tempo, and we are aware of the evolution of our very beings as night turns to another day. Maybe we would live life with a little more urgency, have more fun, and enjoy getting lost as we wander if we lived our lives more truthfully. My connections with people are richer now that I've found a more exposed way of living on two wheels. I love my road family and think about them often as I ride. I'm so happy to be at Sturgis, enjoying their beautiful, fun-loving, rip roaring, unique personalities. I feel safe and free with them.

Today me and the girls crashed this motorcycle club party. We heard there was fancy catered free food, and we were pretty much broke, so we were in! Here at Sturgis we can eat free most every night. I know I can drink for free because the Chrome Cowboys are abundant and they love to treat the Chrome Cowgirls. Mighty gentlemanly.

Good thing I'm hanging with Dena and Connor because I can party all night on Main Street and then cozy up in their amazing digs right on the main drag. They are Sturgis family to me, along with Skip, Cork, Jill, Rusty, Ed, Lori, and so many others.

Saloon 10 in Deadwood is on my mission this trip. I just love that bar. Deadwood is truly a Wild West town. I feel the restless souls of the pioneers and uninhibited cowgirls on the ride between Sturgis and Deadwood. Oh the gold in them thar hills! A Chrome Cowboy I once loved lives here. That boy couldn't tame me, but I wish him the best. I wonder if I'll see him this trip. I'd expected to see him at this party we crashed.

Betsy's off chasing this nice long haired, strapping lad. Gevin and I completely stuffed our faces with free food. We're all famished from the long ride to Sturgis. They came from the west coast, me from the dirty south. I still have road grime on my face, but a fresh coat of lipstick makes it look like a good tan. Tomorrow the Smithsonian Channel will be filming us on our motorcycles riding through the hills. Boy are we gonna give 'em a hoot and hollerin' show.

The Power of Three. Chrome Cowgirls are windsisters forever. Betsy, Me, and Gevin.

camping, playing, exploring off the beaten path, and meeting new folks. We girls get way deep into motorcycle riding, customizing our rides, and spending time together—we're always up for a rip-roaring good time, which basically equals nothing short of sheer bliss and some bad-ass fun memories.

A pack of windsisters are the life of any party, and we create a party everywhere we go. Want to stop traffic? Have a bunch of girls pull up on motorcycles anyplace and time stands still.

Windsisters for Life! The cast of Discovery Channel's *Motorcycle Women* (L-R) Betsy Huelskamp, Qian Ma, Claudia Glenn Barasch, Michelle Dell, Goth Girl, Me.

A windsister will back another sister up when it's time to drop that cheating boyfriend. See how white in the face he goes when three or more femme fatale motorcycle riders encounter the unfaithful fellow. In a man's world, a windsister always has the last word, even if she didn't say anything.

Chick Motolit

Ann Ferrar: *Hear Me Roar*

Dee Gagnon: *DeeTours*

Sara Liberte: *How to Repair and Maintain American V-Twin Motorcycles*

JoAnn Bortles: *How to Custom Paint Your Motorcycle*

Carla King: *Motorcycle Misadventures*

Adele Dubois: *Motorcycle Heat*

Melissa Holbrook Pierson: *The Perfect Vehicle*

Karen Larsen: *Breaking the Limit*

Barbara Jones: *Bike Lust: Harleys, Women, and American Society*

Theresa Wallach: *The Rugged Road*

Jasmine Bluecreek Clark: *Women In The Wind: Fearless Women of the 20th and 21st Centuries*

Fay Taylour: *Queen of the Speed Way*

Christine Firehock: *Christine's KickSTART Motorcycle Training Series*

Doris Maron: *Untamed Spirit*

Carol Setters: *Kick Start: Cosmic Biker Babe's Guide to Life and Changing the Planet*

Jennifer Paterson and Clarissa Dickson Wright: *Two Fat Ladies: Full Throttle*

Erika Lopez: *Flaming Iguanas*

Susie Hollern: *Women in Motorcycling: The Early Years*

Shirley Dicks: *Road Angels: Women Who Ride Motorcycles*

Jean Davidson: *Growing up Harley-Davidson: Memoirs of a Motorcycle Dynasty*

Anything columnist Betsy Huelskamp writes for the magazines

Newsletters from various female motorcycle-riding clubs!

Sasha: *Bikerlady: Living & Riding Free!*

The members in our club are my sisters and my family in every way. The respect and love we all have for each other is just amazing. Our own immediate families would never think about having any kind of gathering without my "sisters." We are there for each other through the good times and bad.

— Bonnie Frankel, President, Cycle Sisters MC

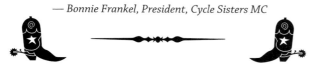

Generally, I'm a lone star, but I love the idea of chick motorcycle clubs where the girls are both the leaders and the followers. We are the spirit of the Valkyries, the combined definition of every Greek and Roman goddess. There are many wonderful all-girl

Danny Ramsey inspires the Chrome Cowgirl in his daughter, Savannah.

clubs; to me that's the perfect place to bond with other riding females. Since I'm more of a lone rider, I prefer not to be affiliated with any one club, but I like to be friends with all of them from around the world. There's a world full of windsisters who ride all kinds of motorcycles, in all different styles. When you are a female motorcycle rider and you meet another chick rider, it's an instant bond. You're soul sisters on the open road . . . or the open track if you're into racing.

WHY GIRLS ARE BETTER RIDERS THAN GUYS

★ Our hips are our power centers, and we belly dance with Hula-Hooping, gyrating grace through the twists and turns.

★ We're gentle with the controls, so we know how to coax our motorcycles through the gears.

★ Straddling a chrome stallion is second nature to us long-rider girls.

Pit Stop Fun

★ Walk into a small-town salon during your journey, all geared up and road grimy after a long ride, wearing your best dirty-girl smile, and go get a manicure and pedicure.

★ When you get off your bike for a resting spell, kick off those riding boots, put on some comfortable, sexy-looking sandals, and enjoy a latté somewhere.

★ Visit a divine spa and treat yourself to a reflexology session where they massage your hands and feet. It's positively mesmerizing, especially after a long ride.

★ Go to the fanciest gym in the area and take a workout. You'll be amazed how powerfully goddess you'll feel when you stride out of that gym and rev up your ride.

★ Make your own web TV show—carry a Flip video camera and create three-minute story chapters of your very own road adventure. Include all the characters you meet along the way and blog about it all, too!

★ Buy one small road treasure at every truck stop or trading post you encounter and exchange these gifts with your windsisters.

★ Ride a mechanical bull two-up and take bets from the spectators on who can ride the longest.

Whether it is a wanderlust or a wonderlust, riding brings out everything sensual and awakens *every* sensation in the rider.

Riding a motorcycle is about going after things. It's about having relentless courage to focus on the moment at hand. It's courage to go beyond boundaries. It's about smoothly going with the flow when there's a twist, having the flexibility to lean with the turn, and being prepared for what's around the bend. This is having *curvaceousness*.

If you didn't ever challenge yourself how would you know what you're capable of? If you know you have the God given ability to do something, but are afraid, then do it afraid.

— Laura Klock, Klock Werks Kustom Cycles and Bonneville Salt Flats motorcycle racer . . .
watch her lick the salt on two wheels!

New York City artist De la Vega speaks the word of the wanderlust soul.

Rocket Science

noun: informal. An endeavor requiring great intelligence or technical ability. (American Heritage Dictionary)

Riding requires mental readiness, and when you ride long enough, being mentally prepared becomes second nature. Scatterbrained living can't happen when you're riding. Savoring the moment and maximizing your drive defines mental readiness.

My motorcycle is my church, and the road is my religion

— Becky Shimek, HelmetHair *magazine.com*

Riding develops confidence in every area of your life, giving you the courage to negotiate those twists and turns that happen on any journey. Motorcycle riding develops mental readiness. Folks often say, "Riding a motorcycle isn't rocket science," to which I say, "Yes, it is rocket science." What the heck is rocket science anyway? Science is about *how, what, when, where,* and *why?* A rocket is jetting off into the atmosphere. A motorcycle is like a rocket; a motorcyclist goes over her preflight checklist before takeoff and then monitors her actions and the technical activities of the vehicle during the voyage, just like an astronaut.

Racing around the track on a chrome horse is like riding a high speed merry-go-round. It is a merry experience to go 'round the track!

Thumbs up after riding in the first ever all Harley-Davidson/Buell Women's Day Ride at Daytona in 2008. The ride featured hundreds of Chrome Cowgirls galloping along the parade route led by Karen Davidson.

THE TWO-WHEELED TANGO

The body and the bike truly tango in an intimate dance as the rider and motorcycle carve asphalt along a mountain pass. The rider's knees pirouette in an "s" turn on the racetrack as the rider leans deep into a curve. Together the Chrome Cowgirl and her chrome horse gallop along, loving and living every single rush of every curvaceous movement. This is the nexus of the soft and tough.

Award-winning motojournalist Genevieve Schmitt captures the epic all-girl ride sponsored by Harley-Davidson/Buell. That's bikebuilder Athena of Vagabond Choppers at the handlebars. Cowgirls love to stunt ride.

Riding at a level high enough to engage in this two-wheeled tango requires a Chrome Cowgirl to develop her riding skills. It means learning advanced riding techniques. There are many terrific books dedicated to developing riding skills, like *Total Control* by Lee Parks and *Ride Hard, Ride Smart* by Pat Hahn, but there are some basic techniques and concepts you should master even before setting out on an advanced riding course.

I pity people who merely exist on this earth instead of truly live in it. The moment we push our machines to the limit we experience a personal freedom. The fact we control them in a world of chaos empowers us to be our own Thelma and Louise.

— *Nika Rolczewski, racer*

BABY, DOES THIS BIKE MAKE MY BUTT LOOK FASTASTIC?

It's good when a Chrome Cowgirl aims to be a bronc buster and tame any style of motorcycle riding. Learning to ride using different techniques only opens up the terrain for new adventure. Sport bike riding and touring provide new ways to carve the canyons and zip along the straightaways.

Shut Up and Race How To's

★ See Shut Up and Ride How To's in Chapter 3 and do all that first.

★ Sign up! Join an association like the AMA (American Motorcyclist Association, www. AMAdirectlink.com) so that you can participate in their enormous race program.

★ Get Power Hungry. Drink in knowledge. Go to track days and take classes at race schools like Super Bike School, Keith Code's R.A.C.E., DMX Women's School of Motocross, Freddie Spencer, Reg Pridmore, or MSF Dirt Bike School, for example. Attend a Femmoto event and pal around the track with powerhouse race girls. Read books and study instructional DVDs.

★ Wear full racing leathers like a James Bond chick and make sure you have an expensive functional full helmet with lots of bad-ass graphics on it.

★ Work out really hard the day before you race so that your adrenaline is pumping when you hit that starting line and you feel absolutely bionic.

Karen Davidson and me at the Harley-Davidson Women's Day Ride. She led hundreds of windsisters through Daytona, parading girl power saddled on powerful chrome horses.

One of the most important concepts to understand when learning to ride aggressively is the concept of the apex. In motorcycling, the apex of a corner is the point when your motorcycle is closest to the inside curve of the turn. The line you select through a corner determines your apex. Generally you want to steer into a turn so that you reach the apex as late as possible. This is because if you hit the apex too early, your angle through the curve will be such that you will run out of your lane and into oncoming traffic. One of the things a good riding course will teach you is to calculate your apex.

I have accomplished a lot in a short amount of time. Success takes time, effort, faith, and determination. Live your own dream and follow your heart! Never ride faster than your angel can fly!

— *Valerie Thompson, Team Owner,*
ValerieThompsonRacing.com

A Chrome Cowgirl Q&A with professional racer and motorcycle safety instructor

THE GLAMOROUS EUROPEAN VICKI "RACEGIRL" GRAY OF MOTORESS, FOUNDER OF INTERNATIONAL FEMALE RIDE DAY, AN ANNUAL EVENT HELD THE FIRST FRIDAY IN MAY

1. Describe the feeling of racing a motorcycle and how it applies to life overall.

Racing a motorcycle is a very natural thing for me—I've always been the type of female who explores activities that take you to the edge, to life's extreme thrills and kicks. Road racing is a challenging activity—not only in the skill set required to manage the machinery but managing the constant danger and risk. It adds spice to this amazing recipe! Managing a mighty powered sport bike through corners, taking off from the starting line with 40 other bikes, all trying to get through the first corner—the adrenaline kick is unbeatable. The use of tactics, ever altering; methods, ever developing; and timing the machinery to maximize every moment—all this is an adventure that never is the same at any split second of the process. The thrills and unimaginable sensations cannot be compared.

2. What would you tell a female rider who wants to race but is a bit fearful, and does racing help to encourage other areas of life?

What I have suggested to women in the past is that before entering into racing, get in some track days. There is a difference between wanting to race and actually being capable of racing. If you get out on the track and find it's for you, then consider getting your race license by taking a course and then going onward from there. If you just jump into racing you might quickly get frustrated, since it's an extremely competitive culture and as much as it gives you the greatest highs, there are lows that really play on your sense of self. These powers have quickly turned even the toughest men away. Racing or motorsport of any kind is a wonderful diversion from life's everyday concerns.

3. How has motorcycling changed your life?

Racing has given me endless new experiences and lessons on so many levels I couldn't possibly begin to define them. I can't say it's changed my life, but rather that it's played a role within the path I'd already chosen. The knowledge I've gathered has been overwhelming. I'm now working on the chance to set land speed records at Bonneville—here I go to explore and understand yet another level of motorcycling.

4. Describe what it is like to witness all these women coming to your Motoress/Racegirl events, and what are the absolute highlights?

It's a most rewarding feeling passing along something to another female motorcyclist that results in a more assured, more pleasurable motorcycling experience. The big reward for me since the day I started teaching back in 1985 has always been when the rider overcomes her (or his, since I've trained many men and still do) fear, her apprehension, and she learns the skill and exclaims: "I've got it!" The excitement and enthusiasm is what fuels me. I've always promoted the fact that the more skills you acquire, the greater the pleasure becomes—the more you know the better it gets.

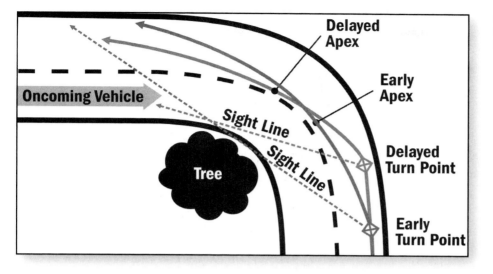

Calculating the apex of a curve is the same as figuring out how the hell you're going to cut through the bullshit and cut to the chase in life. Learning that perfect line that gets you skillfully in and out of a curve is a very thrilling feat, one that delivers excellent results in real-life circumnavigating.

The American Motorcycle Association treasures, adores, and promotes women in motorcycling. Chrome Cowgirls dig the AMA.

FACING FEAR

Racing is the fine art of attaining warp speed on two wheels, maneuvering and managing the body and bike together like one fine unit. Racing is the ultimate fear conqueror because it teaches you

Haley Canoles is an earthy chick who loves to reach for the sky. *Courtesy of Haley Canoles*

Motocross racers don't tiptoe through life, nor do we walk along the edge; we run along the edge jumping and dodging anything that gets in our way. "Mediocre" is a word that we know nothing about.

— Haley "Holy Cannoli" Canoles, WMA #873

146

how to manage fear without hitting the panic button. Fear. What to do with this little devilish feeling that creeps into you when you're on the verge of experiencing something new, fun, and exciting?

If you go past your fear, oh my, what a landscape you'll discover. Your whole world opens up. When we face our fear, we seek a higher power within ourselves. We may crave speed in our bones. We may even have a few speeding tickets to prove our infatuation with going fast. If you start riding too fast, you need to take it to the track, set that bike up to race, and really see how your pony performs.

I love race instructor Keith Code's books. In *Twist of the Wrist*, which provides in-depth instruction in racing technique and basic good motorcycle operating skill, Code talks about the economy of fear and how it eats up your attention span and concentration. Is he ever right! He talks about spending your attention wisely when riding, and these tidbits can be applied to life, too. Think of how panic and fear just destroy self-confidence, trust, and goals. Attention span and concentration happen *in the moment*. Fear is something that can't exist in a moment because fear is emotively predicting a negative future episode or emotively dwelling on a negative past scenario brought into the fun at hand. So fearing something might happen, or fear about something that did happen, or just simply fear from lack of self-confidence, will devour precious full-throttle energy and remove a rider from the moment. That's no fun.

GETTIN' DOWN AND DIRTY

I consider myself an Earthy Chick. I love running my hands deep into the soil when I garden. I love the smell of dirt. Thus dirt biking is right up my alley. Powering over terrain and popping wheelies is playtime in the dirt. Doing it in the dirt is a lesson that improves your street riding skills, preparing you for inevitable encounters with debris in the road, gravel, unstable roads, and varmints skittering in front of you. You learn how to masterfully tackle those obstacles so smoothly, it's as if those obstacles weren't even there.

Dirt-bike riding is like gardening. You seed the tire against the earth. You blossom as you conquer dirty terrain. Dirt-bike riding to me is like the essence of a renaissance festival. You blaze a trail

FUEL FOR THOUGHT
DO IT IN THE DIRT. If you want to learn to become a better street rider, go to dirt-bike school and learn how to be a dirty rider. Then you'll learn the finer art of picking up a dropped bike, whooping it up, falling down and getting back in the saddle again, and beating any obstacle that gets in your way.

through the forest like a woodland nymph. Doing it in the dirt requires mud, guts, and glory, and that's what an Earthy Chick is all about when she blazes trails.

The joy of tackling the landscape and maneuvering the dirt bike to mount virtually anything in its path reminds me of the capability of surmounting any obstacle, hidden or obvious, blocking the intended path of travel. Indeed I think motocross and trials riding forces the rider to negotiate, so tactics are developed, and you can carry those lessons into real life. Playing in the dirt can teach a rider a lot of things. Cowgirls had to guide their horses through and around harrowing situations that tested the spirit of animal and rider. Riding in the dirt and skillfully planning one's choreography through the forest or on the dirt track develops a rodeo talent that we can use audaciously in real-life dirty situations.

Chick Motoflicks and Other Inspiring Motorcycle Movies

* Thelma & Louise
* Girl on a Motorcycle
* Chopper Chicks from Hell
* Motorcycle Women
* Biker Women
* She Lives to Ride
* The Motorcycle Diaries (the film based on the life of Che Guevara)
* Motorcycle Diaries (the documentary by Diane Howells)

* Girls from Thunder Strip
* The Mini-Skirt Mob
* Angels' Wild Women
* Easy Rider
* Wild at Heart
* Torque
* Me & Will
* Girl Gone Bad

Road Diary:

Sturgis really celebrates the competitive rider. There are all kinds of races and competitions that make me want to pick something and become good at it. I love going fast, but I think I like things like motocross where you get to ride in the dirt. I have a love for it all so in order to find out which style of Racey Jane I'll be best at, I'm just going to take classes in every style of competition and figure out which one suits me. These will be dollars well spent because I'll be able to really ride the heck out of a motorcycle beyond the street. I can take all that I learn and maximize my motorcycle's potential and increase my riding abilities, all while having tons of fun and meeting new riders. Now I'll really be immersed in my passion. Though I'm inseam challenged and these sport bikes are tall for little me, I'm gonna find a way to make it work. Maybe I'll pioneer something new and open up a whole new territory for us short girls. In the meanwhile, I'm heading for the hills—the AMA hill-climb competition that is—a place where a vertically challenged girl can reach new heights by riding straight up the side of a mountain on her motorcycle.

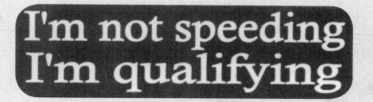

I'm not speeding I'm qualifying

WIDE OPEN TIL YOU SEE GOD —THEN BRAKE —

Two Hearts and a Hart on fire with the passion for motorcycle riding. Me with legendary female motorcycle icon Malysa Wyse and Discovery Channel bike builder and Chrome Cowboy Jay Hart of Chop Smiths. *English Jim*

Never be intimidated by anything in life.

— Amanda Overmyer, American Idol finalist, season seven (2008), and in-home medical nurse

Route 7
GIRLS RIDE OUT

Partying at the rallies and fundraiser events is the ultimate "girls ride out." Rallies and events are pack-wild family reunions where you meet up with all your riding pals from all over the country. A rally is a place where friends can let it all hang out and toast one another, celebrating freedom on the open road. I've seen regular folks who lead pretty consistent lives as corporate executives get wild and daring at the rallies. It's refreshing to see because these are the people you deal with every day—bank staffers, insurance people, lawyers, and doctors, for instance. You also get to meet all the unique, happy-go-lucky individuals who live their lives out loud every day and never curb their enthusiasm for a moment due to social or corporate demands. Sometimes I think that's the reason why so many regular people now ride—they want some of what us Chrome Cowgirls got: freedom and individuality.

GIVE TO RIDE, RIDE TO GIVE:
THE ALTRUISTIC SOUL

Chrome Cowgirls have Texas-sized hearts. This is evident in the way they always look after others. That is the motorcycle mama in them;

Nothing ever happened in the past; it happened in the Now. Nothing will ever happen in the future; it will happen in the Now.

— *Eckart Tolle,* The Power of Now

Getting dirty in the dirty South at the Smoke Out Rally. Me with the crew from Music City Motorcycles.

whenever there's a fundraiser, you can be sure that there'll be a pack of girl motorcycle riders galloping in on all kinds of chrome stallions and mares to support a good cause. Some even bring baked goods in their saddlebags. Yes, the Chrome Cowgirl is soft but tough to the core.

LIFE IS A PARTY, AND I'M GONNA RIDE IT ALL LIFE LONG!

We carry that rally feeling in us all year long; the rally sense of adventure and celebration bubbles in our hearts and souls, and we can draw on the memories anytime we need some strength and power. Our rally experiences influence the way we walk, talk, contemplate, and handle our everyday lives. We live life full throttle on a full tank of gas. Because of our road mentality, we are able to step back and take a good long look at things the way we truly see them, rather than through the filter of everyone else's eyes. Living life like it is something to look forward to every day is to ride a life filled with intense meaning.

Riding is like listening to a great song. Music just takes you to that riding feeling, even when you're standing still.

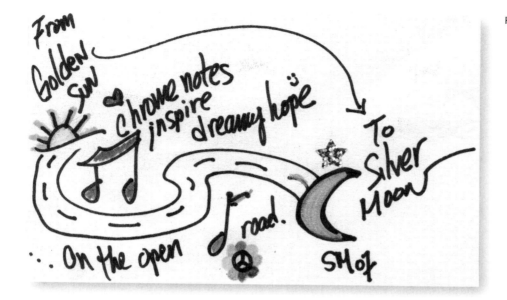

From Golden Sun chrome notes inspire dreamy hope ...On the open road. To Silver Moon SMof

The website www.motorcycleevents.com provides a list of all kinds of motorcycle riding celebrations around the globe.

MOTORCYCLE MUSIC

"Great music makes you lose yourself, abandon your environment and merge with the sound," says Bob Lefsetz, music industry analyst. To me, motorcycles are forever representative of a free-spirited renaissance in which you can lose yourself, abandon your routine environment, and merge with the rhythm of the road again and again.

Riding a motorcycle is like listening to a vinyl record with all its pops and skips. It makes your heart skip a beat or two while you trust that warm sound of the motor humming between your legs. It's just like the way a good song will bare your soul and leave your heart nude and your mind a little restless for more—that's riding, that's what the rhythm of the road will do to a passionate rider out there on just two wheels cruising along miles of asphalt ribbon.

The rallies and events make for a perfect occasion to make lasting memories and to give your heart a much-needed lift.

FUEL FOR THOUGHT

Ride It Like Ya Stole It... Don't look for me, baby, I've disappeared in the wind. I'm a rockin' and a rollin' down the highway, motorin' to places I've never been... trippin' off to paradise. Some will call me crazy, but I don't care. I love to rock it... I love to roll it... I love to ride my motorcycle like I stole it!

<blockquote>

**Never be intimidated by anything in life;
always go right ahead with what you're doing.
For me, riding is the freedom and ability to get
on the bike and just cruise alone. The silence
of the wind is empowering.**

— Amanda Overmyer, American Idol *finalist, season seven (2008),
and in-home medical nurse*

</blockquote>

Being the music junkie that I am, here's a partial list of excellent favorites

(IF I INCLUDED A COMPLETE LIST OF ROADWORTHY CHROME COWGIRL TUNES, IT WOULD FILL HALF THE BOOK)

1234 — Feist
Ain't Nothin' but a She Thing — Salt-N-Pepa
Amelia — Joni Mitchell
America — Gloria Gaynor
Attitude — Wynonna Judd
Better Be Good to Me — Tina Turner
Biker Chick — Jo Dee Messina
Bitch — Meredith Brooks
Born to Fly — Sara Evans
Bye, Bye Baby — Janis Joplin
Come Away With Me — Norah Jones
Control — Janet Jackson
Cornflake Girl — Tori Amos
Cry on the Shoulder of the Road — Martina McBride
Destiny — Zero 7
Elsewhere — Sarah McLachlan
Express Yourself — Madonna
Fade into You — Mazzy Star
Finding My Way Back Home — Lee Ann Womack
Free — Sarah Brightman

Freeway of Love — Aretha Franklin
Get Right with God — Lucinda Williams
Get the Party Started — Pink
Go Your Own Way — Fleetwood Mac
God Shiva — Me'shell Ndegéocello
Good As Gone — Little Big Town
Groove Is in the Heart — Deee-lite
Gypsies, Tramps and Thieves — Cher
Here for the Party — Gretchen Wilson
Holla Back Girl — Gwen Stefani
I'm So Excited — Pointer Sisters
In My Imagination — Patti Scialfa
Independent Women — Destiny's Child
It's My Life — No Doubt
Jesus Take the Wheel — Carrie Underwood
Joyride — Jennifer Hanson
Kick It Out — Heart
Last Train to Clarksville — Cassandra Wilson
Little Bird — Annie Lennox
Little Wing — Concrete Blonde

We're all in this together. Family and friends are one and the same at motorcycle rallies and events. The only reason you don't see Sara Liberte in this photo is because she's snapping this shot. l-r JoAnn, me, Cindy, Betsy, Candy, Gevin
Sara Liberte

Looking for Answers — Susan Tedeschi
Make It Happen — Mariah Carey
Middle of the Road — The Pretenders
Midnight Rider — Patti Smith
Miss Independent — Kelly Clarkson
Motorcycle Mama — Neil Young & Nicolette Larson
Never Alone — Barlow Girl
Not Gonna Turn Back — Jasmine Cain
On the Road Again — Katie Melua
Open Your Eyes, You Can Fly — Vanessa Williams
Rhythm of Life — Paula Cole
Ride — Shelly Fairchild
Right to Be Wrong — Joss Stone
Rock N Roll N Motorcycle Soul — Sasha and
   Motoroadeo M/C
Rock This Country — Shania Twain
Runaway — Deee-Lite
Running Up That Hill — Kate Bush
Shameless — Ani DiFranco
So Many Stars — Kathleen Battle

St. Teresa — Joan Osborne
Steve McQueen — Sheryl Crow
Strength, Courage, Wisdom — India.Arie
Super Fly — Four Non Blondes
To Zion — Lauryn Hill
The Long Way Around — The Dixie Chicks
The Road's My Middle Name — Bonnie Raitt
The Wanderer — Donna Summer
The Wheel — Rosanne Cash
Thelma and Louise — Trish Murphy
Travelin' Thru — Dolly Parton
U.N.I.T.Y. — Queen Latifah
We Are Family — Sister Sledge
What I Am — Edie Brickell
Whatever Way the Wind Blows — Kelly Willis
Where Will I Be? — Emmylou Harris
Yes I Am — Melissa Etheridge
You Gotta Be — Des'ree
You Learn — Alanis Morrisette
Your Good Girl Is Gonna Go Bad — Tammy Wynette

The Chrome Cowgirl ABCs to Live By, Part Deux
(IF THE FIRST ALPHABET WASN'T ENOUGH, WELL HERE'S SOME MORE)

★ **A—AWARE.** All the senses become fully alive and aware and you feel positively bionic.

★ **B—BOLD.** A woman on her motorcycle is a bold character, ready to seize the day and all its stories.

★ **C—CHARACTER.** The distinctive qualities of her personality finally burst forth, encouraged by a weekend motorcycle camping trip that brought her true character out to play.

★ **D—DAYDREAM.** Saddled on her ride with a few good hours of riding time, she felt like she was flying; this was a dream experienced while awake during the day.

★ **E—ENCOURAGE.** The motorcycle encourages a rider to fulfill unrealized dreams and summon lost passion back into the heart and soul of the rider.

★ **F—FAR-REACHING.** Our two-wheeled motorized freedom machines deliver us into the far reaches of body, mind, and soul, taking us to a moment when there is nothing but the rush of the wind and the knowledge that we are related to a far-reaching God that reaches out to bring us closer to our truth.

★ **G—GENTLE.** The art of riding a motorcycle is an act of gently and gracefully maneuvering the controls, thus acquiring a riding skill that is second nature. It's sort of like the grace needed to run skillfully in stiletto heels.

★ **H—HANG IN THERE.** Hang in There. It's what we do when we go the distance on our motorcycles trying to find answers in the wind. It's also what we tell ourselves to do when work sucks and we want to be out riding.

★ **I—INDEPENDENCE.** She was confident in herself and her abilities as she maintained her independence and took off on her own motorcycle with a T-shirt that said "If You Can Read This, The Bitch Got Her Own." This was a response to the T-shirt slogan referencing the female passenger that reads: "If You Can Read This, The Bitch Fell Off."

★ **J—JUSTICE.** "Justice once, would you stop calling my cell phone so that I can finish my day tripping," she huffed to her son as she started her motorcycle after filling up.

★ **K—KICK-START.** She decided to kick-start her life and finally buy that motorcycle, when nothing else seemed to do.

★ **L—LIBERTY.** A girl on a motorcycle is a picture of liberty.

★ **M—METAMORPHIC.** Like a butterfly emerging from her cocoon, the female motorcycle rider enters a metamorphic stage in her life and is free to be herself forever.

★ **N—NOW.** No need to wait to embrace your freedom. Ride now. Dream now. Go for it, right now.

* *O*—**ODD.** She was odd, as in slightly greater than even, in the way she customized her motorcycle, leaving the dude bike builders in awe.

* *P*—**PRIORITY.** When a female motorcycle rider runs down her list of what's priority, postponing a motorcycle ride is rarely an option.

* *Q*—**QUICK.** A girl who loves to ride is quick to say "no" when her boss asks if she'll stay late; she's planning on rising early to greet that sun as she tears down the road on the first mile of her motorcycle journey.

* *R*—**ROLL MODEL.** Ever see what happens when a girl on a motorcycle rolls into a gas station: everybody's eyes fall upon her. What do they see? A portrait of freedom, a symbol of liberty, an untamed spirit embracing her role as the perfect model of her being.

* *S*—**SUPERB.** Women motorcycle riders are superb at advanced riding techniques and adapting to new riding adventures.

* *T*—**TANGO.** Those curves twisting and turning, dipping and diving, ebbing and flowing, this is the daring tango between rider and her motorcycle, dancing the road fantastic.

* *U*—**UNTAMED.** There is never a need to tame that which cannot be held back, and a girl with a quick throttle response is like a bird in flight.

* *V*—**VALUED.** She values life, which is in such short and limited supply, and she valued her motorcycle that gives her a better quality of life.

* *X*—**XANADU.** She found her Xanadu, her stately pleasure dome, out in the Badlands, watching the sun set in a fiery glow.

* *Y*—**YOUTHFUL.** A girl on a motorcycle is forever ageless because riding is about being youthful and innocent, almost childlike as we embrace thrill-seeking playtime on the wide-open road.

* *Z*—**ZOOM.** "Zoom time," she said to her friends as she kick-started the old Panhead, maneuvered her chopper away from the parked bikes on Main Street, and zoomed off. "Zoom time," she whispered in her helmet as the green flag snapped low and the bikes zoomed off the starting line.

The Fryed Brothers at the Knuckle Saloon. The biker band of all biker bands.

Left: Bike night at the Hard Rock Café, NYC, sponsored by Indian Larry Legacy.

My windsister Jasmine Cain drives the crowds wild with her high-octane performance at the Broken Spoke Saloon. *Kelli Heidler*

Entertaining rally folk and friends in my Chrome Leathers at the Broken Spoke Saloon. *Michael Lichter*

Left: Bean're, the motorcycle mayor of everywhere and one of my favorite Chrome Cowboys!

Right: Lex Gray is a motorcyclin' singin' Chrome Cowgirl from NYC.

The Sturgis family gets bigger every year.

There's a wonderful time to be had with the guys from Harley-Davidson France and Erik Buell.

Jay Allen, the host and owner of the World's Biggest Biker Bar, the Broken Spoke Saloon, knows how to throw the best parties! *Courtesy of Jay Allen*

Chrome Cowgirl's pitstop in NYC was the legendary CBGBs.

Rockin' the block with friends in Nashville.

Left: Me with some legendary Chrome Cowgirls and Iron Butt riders. (Left-to-right: Sasha, Phyllis Lang, author Dee Gagnon, Mary Sue)

Right: Taming the Ice Cream Man from Hell's loose tongue.

Here are some wonderful Harley-Davidson dealer folks having a good time in Nashville during the dealer convention. Yes, of course, that's the one and only New York Myke Shelby, owner of San Diego Harley-Davidson—Mr. Life of the Party (2nd from right)

New directions have opened up in my life because of my passion for motorcycles. It began innocently enough, but attraction turned to infatuation after I bought my first bike. The sheer physicality of riding awakens every one of my senses—sight, sound, smell, taste, and touch. The heightening of my senses combined with the speed and power I feel when I'm on the road have given me courage to take giant leaps of faith, and to create a more-beautiful life than I've ever dreamed of. Before I left on my first ride to Sturgis, I took a leave of absence from my high-powered corporate career. The day after I got home, I put my house on the market and vowed never to return to that soulless job. That magical ride to Sturgis crystallized what I wanted to do with my life. It helped me realize my dream of living and working in the motorcycle world. I never looked back—I only wonder what took me so long?

— *Marjorie "Shadow" Kleiman,*
Editor, Thunder Press–North Edition

Betsy likes to call us "road hags." Gevin likes to think of us as "saddle tramps." I stick to Chrome Cowgirls.

Betsy knows how to handle the law. She makes her own rules and then tells those rules to the cops, who usually oblige this Chrome Cowgirl.

Road Journal:

This morning I volunteered to work my friend Darcy Betlach's Biker's Breakfast event at the Broken Spoke Saloon. She's a powerful motorcycle riding executive and is the queen of marketing in the industry. Darcy has a big heart and is brilliant at creating opportunities to raise awareness for those less fortunate, and to celebrate the artists of our culture who build bikes and have other motorcycle riding talents. I checked in all the media folks attending the event. Amazing how the motorcycle business is now like the entertainment business, with celebrities and all kinds of formalities. Soon there will be a red carpet complete with fashion analysts and black tie award ceremonies on major networks. It's gotten that Hollywood!

Speaking of Hollywood, I filmed today for the new Smithsonian Channel. My beautiful windsister buddy Betsy invited me to join in the fun, along with Genevieve Schmitt and Gevin Fax. Wowzee. Talk about a powerful bunch of chick riders in the business. Genevieve had to cut out early because she was doing some other event, so it was just the three wild chicks: me, Gevin, and Betsy. We gave them a lens full! The producer and crew were great fun, very accommodating and professional. They certainly knew what they wanted and so easily and quickly communicated to us all film directions, which we pumped to number eleven in presentation. I still had my filthy bug gut windshield on my chopper. I mean, I wanted to take it off because it so messes up filming, but, at the same time, it's so me to ride with a windshield because I do ride with one all over the country. Windshields reduce unsightly wrinkles from wind burn. Plus, my skin is saved from being pelted by rain and fat June bugs splattering on my fair Irish skin.

We had to do a great deal of canyon riding. All three of us worked those twists and turns in unison, like we were a three-part harmony in perfect pitch. By the end of the filming, we were just grinning ear to ear. I handed them my demo CD and told them to just pop it in and enjoy it as a soundtrack for the day. They loved it and asked if they may use some of the songs as soundtrack! Yeah!

Betsy talked a local police officer out of giving the film crew a ticket for being so precariously perched out of their minivan while they filmed us. We roared with laughter over that. She seduced the uniformed boy. Betsy now knows every cop in Sturgis. Gevin is like Xena, the warrior princess, since she's a high school gym teacher and is all muscle. She's breathtakingly beautiful in her soul and in her physical presence. She's smart and fun and can ride the hell out of a motorcycle. Gevin also wrenches on her own bikes. She's fashionable, too. Her and Betsy have the riding wardrobe thing down. After the Smithsonian filming, we hustled over to Michael Lichter's incredible exhibit at Thunder Road. That was another fun industry event. I celebrate this artist's photojournalism. No one can capture the motorcycle lifestyle quite like Mike Lichter. It is an honor to have been photographed by this legendary artist. Our passion for riding has made us all dear friends for life.

My beloved, who rode up on a Heritage Springer and whisked me off into the most roamantic sunset for life.

If you are going to doubt something, doubt your limits.

— Don Ward

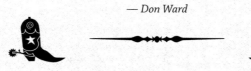

Route 8
ROAMANTIC
Nomadic Love:
Chrome Cowboys and Chrome Charmings

Having a lover who gets the motorcycle thing is 75 percent of an amazing relationship. Sharing a love for riding and being free spirits together is a gift beyond measure. If you worship the freedom in the other, nagging is not in your vocabulary *except* if your lover promised to help change your oil in your bike 'cause you're working, and he or she did not do that because they went to catch wind for themselves. Then some nagging might surface.

A good Chrome Cowboy knows how to be the perfect suitor because besides wooing a Chrome Cowgirl, his agenda includes giving that girl a lot of space to be herself. He encourages her and brings out the very best in his girl, as she does in him. He's not going to tell her to act a

---

Chrome Cowboy

Got my eye on a prize he stands about 6'2"
Strapping fine man, mmm, head to toe tattoos
He wears black leather worn rough
From highway history, oh he's tough
Got arms the size of my legs and I beg him to give me a ride.
Chrome Cowboy don't you know you drive me wild
The way you ride your motorcycle bronco style
Acting like you're one tough son of a gun,
I think you know and I know we could have big fun . . .

© copyright 2006 Road Diva Music Ascap

certain way, and he'll never say, "Why you gotta ride that thing?" Nope, he'll be as proud as a man could ever be when he sees his queen of the highway saddle up and ride away on her adventure. Why, he might even surprise you when you call him from that Harley dealership to let him know you're pit stopping. Next thing you know, there's a sales lady following you out the door asking if you're Ms. So and So because there's a hundred-dollar gift certificate waiting for you.

How to Be a Chrome Cowgirl Biker Bride

Getting married biker style has got to be one of the most fun and exciting methods of exchanging nups. Here's the top-ten rundown for getting married biker style:

1. It's sexy and romantic, and your Chrome Charming will forever remember you as this blushing biker chick.

2. You get to wear a white bikini and veil, or any other unique bridal outfit you can dream up, which makes for a merry wedding that's a dream!

3. Your wedding will be the best honky-tonk, rip-roaring throw-down possible, one that your friends will remember for years to come.

4. The wedding celebration lasts for the duration of the rally, and then your anniversary celebrations can be an annual rally event!

5. Everyone can come dressed up like Chrome Cowboys and Chrome Cowgirls.

6. The banquet can be at places like Saloon 10 in Deadwood, the Wreck in Daytona, or the Broken Spoke Saloon in Laconia, for instance.

7. The wedding ceremony can be high atop the Black Hills in Sturgis, on the beach, at the Speedway at Daytona Bike Week, or in the backyard of a Harley-Davidson dealership; it can be just about anywhere a motorcycle can go. The world is a wide-open road for weddings.

8. Your honeymoon can be the two of you riding off into the sunset on a most romantic road trip to all the sensual destinations you can dream about like under the stars in a desert campground, at a spa, at a bed and breakfast, in a cabin, or at a resort.

9. Don't go over 30 miles per hour with a veil on your head, or else it'll look like the bottom of Lily Munster's dress. And make sure you wear a tiara-style veil so that everyone knows that you are queen.

10. If you wear a bikini as your white wedding outfit, be sure to wear a pretty white sarong with it because you don't want all these people staring at your butt while you speak your sacred words.

Me and my Chrome Charming. I found him at last! A fairy tale featuring two Harley-Davidson motorcycles and their musical riders. *Julie Martin*

A Chrome Cowboy shares in your enthusiasm for adventure and discovery. He wants you to follow your dreams and reach beyond any boundaries. That fellow is excited about your tall tales on the open road. He loves the nomad in you.

Likewise, a Chrome Cowgirl will completely W.O.W. (with out words) understand a Chrome Cowboy's life in every way, if

**If you are going to doubt something,
doubt your limits.**

— *Don Ward*

Tattoo artist Brandon Hanna of Nashville Lone Wolf Tattoo Parlor and his missus.

he treats her right and gives her freedom and encouragement. Anytime a chrome cowboy tries to take away any of those virtues, why that chrome is dropped right off his title and he is then called coward boy. A strong man stands behind his Chrome Cowgirl. She wouldn't have it any other way. He's got to hold his own and be his own man, not rely upon her so that he can feel like he has some sort of life. No, the perfect Chrome Cowboy walks tall in any crowd and can handle almost any situation like a strappin' fine man can.

The Chrome Cowboy is a spirited man, too, wise and humble, yet a force of delicious everything.

A GALLERY OF ONLY SOME OF MY FAVORITE CHROME COWBOYS

Left: The Triumph chopper man Michael Kramer. Give this Chrome Cowboy any type of motoproject, and he'll turn it into a triumphant work of art.

Right: Erik Buell with Mike Stone of Queensryche and the Peavy Guitar Buell designed, which combines guitar technology with motor technology to create one bad axe. Not only can Erik mastermind bikes, you ought to see his chops on guitar. *Courtesy of Erik Buell*

English Jim gives a new meaning to photojournalism. He captures those photos you had no idea were taken of you.

My favorite builder, legendary character, and multi-talented artist, my dear friend, Indian Larry, R.I.P. His legacy lives on forever. *Bobby Seeger, Jr.*

Left: Bob Kay is truly one of my very favorite motorcycle-business Chrome Cowboys. He supports Chrome Cowgirls and champions their desire to have more products to customize and max out their riding experience.

Right: Cactus, a true highway hero.

Left: Conner Sheets leads many curious film crews on motorcycle rally TV shoots through the vast South Dakota landscape, saddled on his Iron Horse.

Right: Gasper Trauma taught me to ride, along with other staff members from his school (second from left).

Left: Stephen Ransom is so passionate about motorcycles that not only does he build bikes, he creates art work out of all kinds of motorcycle parts.

Right: Charlie St. Clair is the Laconia Motorcycle Rally executive director. How about his road jeans and jacket? Charlie has road stories to tell!

Left: Paul Cox is a brilliant craftsman and leather artisan. An artistic brother to the legendary Indian Larry, he carries on the legacy of his beloved friend.

Right: Is that thunder I hear, the *Cycle Source?* Editor Chris Callen guns the throttle of that fun magazine that truly captures the essence of the culture.

Former Indian Larry legacy builder Keino in Times Square.

Rodent is always scurrying about, capturing the motorcycle rally lifestyle with his unique journalism talents.

Left: My Santa's got a fleet of reindeer motorcycles that pull his sled.

Right: Chris Sorensen, guitarist for Motoroadeo M/C, can imitate the sound of a roaring Harley on his slide guitar with throttle-response precision.

Panhead Phil of Music City Motorcycles with his son, Chase. Panhead is ol skool all the way. *Photo by Shaun Silva*

Rick Fairless is a champion business man and builder of fine motorcycles. An inspiration to many.

Three of the most amazing Chrome Cowboys, all with a special place in my heart, l-r Danny Gray, Dave Nichols, Mark Howlett. *Michael Lichter*

Left: Fred "Scout" has an unending love affair with the open road on his motorcycle.

Right: Skip MacLeod and I are like peas and carrots at the rallies and on the road of life.

Left: The Captain. Peter Fonda makes a speech at the Motorcycle Hall of Fame Breakfast in Sturgis. He is an all-time legendary Chrome Cowboy.

Right: Willie of Tropical Tattoo in Daytona hosts one of the best ol' skool bike shows during bike week. His shop also created my Tigerlily tattoo. *English Jim*

Left: Ed and his wife Vera own the legendary motorcycle pit stop the Rock Store in Cornell, California.

Right: Chris Maida is one of the happiest Chrome Cowboys I have ever met.

Left: Master bike builder Cyril Huze encourages everyone to follow their dreams.

Right: Bandit KRB is my mentor and friend, a very special person who always encourages my art.

Film producer and director of film photography, John Beymer with me and Betsy. John scouts for film locations upon his Harley Davidson.

Left: Former Senator Ben Nighthorse Campbell rides his chrome stallion all the way to Washington, D.C., for the annual Rolling Thunder motorcycle event honoring veterans.

Right: Sheriff Speed Finlay is a refugee from the Wild West days of the chrome cowboy.

Left: My Patrick built this Harley-Davidson-themed bass.

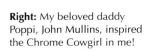

Right: My beloved daddy Poppi, John Mullins, inspired the Chrome Cowgirl in me!

Niko on his "Barfly."

Blowing kisses goodbye. My driveway leads me to and from a vast world of asphalt ribbon upon which to chase dreams and ride the winds of adventure. *Skip Macleod*

QUEEN'S SEAT: AN UNINTERRUPTED VIEW FOR THE PASSENGER

Sometimes this Chrome Cowgirl loves to be a passenger. That uninterrupted view from behind, sitting high on the pillion pad, experiencing a sheer transcendence with rider and ride, can be summed up in one word: *riderotica*. A hot man and a roaring engine between my legs are some compensation for those times when I must ride two-up on a motorcycle. Two-up riding into the sunset on a chrome horse is one of the most *roam*antic scenes a girl can experience—just the two of you and the motorcycle swiftly galloping along the pavement.

Being a passenger offers an uninterrupted view that allows your mind to wander. When I'm a passenger, I completely absorb the scenery, leaning deep into my Chrome Cowboy's back to communicate some lovely thoughts while we ride. Riding as a passenger, zoning out to the sound of the wind while dreamily connecting with the landscape, lets my soul wander way out there lost (and at the same time found) in divine thought, something that's not possible when I'm at the handlebars driving. Riding pillion is pure motomeditation for the passenger; a very carefree experience.

FUEL FOR THOUGHT

Riding a motorcycle is a psychedelic experience, a natural high. *Psychedelic,* according to the *Random House Dictionary,* is: "a mental state characterized by a profound sense of intensified sensory perception." Oh yeah, baby, riding is the ultimate psychedelic high.

Road Diary:

I love all motorcycles. They're like fine horses. I even love scooters. They're like ponies. But, I must say that seeing the H-D label excites me in a more profound way. The brand lets me know that I'm part of something large and amazing—the way God invites you into the fold.

The core H-D riders are a fold of wayward sheep looking for a deeper experience of pleasure and reality, of truth and beauty, the essence of the individual! Life and riding as art. The bike coaxes out the truth. Why do so many people tattoo the Harley brand on their bodies? Because the brand celebrates the free spirit, the uninhibited soul; it celebrates life as art and therefore all the unique traits of individuals.

Riding a motorcycle is living out loud, so, thanks to H-D for the constant encouragement. The Harley-Davidson brand encourages a rider to go, seek, be, explore, serve, love, experience, connect, forgive, understand, ride, hope, to discover that life is an adventure. Seek and you shall find—trust, laugh, and be. Everything good happens on a Harley. Everything amazing happens on two wheels. Period. No matter what you ride.

Before departing from the rally, I stopped by to see Dan Rinerson for acupuncture healing to keep my energy totally and clearly aligned with the pulse of the Black Hills. I discovered that tapping deeply into the spiritual experience of Sturgis and the Black Hills is one of the most important aspects of experiencing this rally.

The next morning, I packed up my bike and departed my friend Lori's cozy little house in Rapid City. The air temperature had already started to climb, and I knew triple digit temps were a mere hour away.

Yep, I had heat exhaustion from the extreme heat and had to grab a Super 8. I couldn't even camp out. I needed to relax in the air conditioning and cool my overheated body. Never in my years of riding solo or passenger have I experienced such effects from the heat; then again, I can't remember riding in such heat. But never mind this unbearable heat; this is living because I'm out here riding free! I just need to find me a place to chill out for a while!

One dude told me that standing still on his bike, it was 116 degrees. Holy cow! In addition to the asphalt oven below the wheels and the sun roasting the oxygen, the engine cooks you. It took me much longer to get home than expected. Like a day and a half more! I had to cut my mileage way down and stop a lot more to drink water. This meant I just met more cool people because I had the time to shoot the breeze with them. I dehydrated super fast, even though I was wearing a light colored long sleeve shirt. My darling Chrome Charming, Patrick, was so coolly refreshing, and I wanted to climb through the telephone and curl up in his bear huggin' arms. With his calming South Carolina drawl, he coaxed me home through that unbearable heat! A man who encourages my free spirit to soar is a definite keeper! I treasure and positively adore him!

Now I'm pulling into my driveway. My driveway . . . my own little piece of asphalt heaven. I celebrate my driveway. It opens out and leads me to a vast world and takes me up to the front door of my nest when I return from my adventures.

When I return home, I utter words of thanks for having been able to shut up and ride and let the journey unfold for me. And sometimes that ain't easy. But I learned that to let go and get up and go, that's living. That's when I feel alive. Yes, after a long journey, I feel I've added a new Chrome Cowgirl chapter to my life story. I love the adventure. Riding has given me the gift of waking every day inspired and connected to Mother Earth and all her inhabitants. It has given me a vast capacity to feel thankful to God for another day in the Chrome Cowgirl life.

Road inspired art by Sasha

Upon reaching your destination, you may be tempted to light a cigarette because the passenger experience was, yes, that good. All the senses come alive as you tear down the highway. He reaches back and squeezes your calf, so you scooch yourself closer to him so you can breathe in his scent and get lost in the moment.

When you abandon all the things that aren't working for you like ugly relationships and decide to seek another way of living, that's when you learn to love life. Just love that journey no matter what.

THE FREE WAY: A NO-EXCUSE APPROACH TO GRABBING LIFE BY THE HANDLEBARS AND LIVING A FREER LIFESTYLE!

If we never venture past the small boundaries that lace our everyday lives, we'll never know our full potential. Ever. One day, we'll wake up at some random moment and realize that the path was always there, waiting, but we were just too damn skeptical to really take that first step.

Desert Oasis

And I ride my two-wheeled freedom machine
To this place where freedom is learned and burned
Upon the heart of woman,
Vast and far reaching with heaven above speaking.

The land is stark and dry here, and it is void of any season.
The wind brought me here to this desert oasis.
Traveling miles through lush territory, colorful, it now skews my reason
So that I can communicate with the Source of all Being.

The roar of the engine is vibrating a new song, and my soul is hungry for more,
So I drive out of the comfort zone of all that I know and abandon
The world wellspring that always leaves me dying of thirst,
And I drink of a new adventure and taste the sand of time on my tongue.

by Sasha © Lovechild Writes 2007

One happy rider. *English Jim*

My true path was always there, waiting for me, but I took another path that seemed safer with less risk. That's what I was taught to do, and fear made me stay put because I was afraid of disappointing my family. A job with benefits was the path of least resistance. Because I had been so radically different from my peers and family growing up, I couldn't have cared less about the stale job with benefits. I craved the adventure of living free on the open road, but this was unacceptable for my family. I didn't want to rock the boat.

But I kept dreaming of other paths into the wild and unknown, where I belonged! It lured my gypsy soul—my musical soul, my artistic soul—much more than the safe path presented by the corporate world.

Solitude is the audience chamber of God.

— Walter Savage Lander

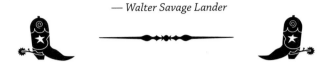

My true path waited for a long time, until I could no longer stand the phony path I was on. It was totally opposed to my wild-child nature. The curious artist inside of me, this nomadic gypsy spirit, was a prisoner on the tidy path of false certainty. Finally it was time to take the journey, time to be true, no matter what, so I turned my wheels, cut across the woods, and headed onto that overgrown, mysterious path that was my reality.

On my true path, my world burst alive. The earth came to life. A rainbow tasted sweet, like a fruit bowl. The rain washed away the old, making way for the new. The trees danced. The wind blew away the cobwebs from musty thinking. And my two-wheeled freedom machine freed my mind from thought so I could just be engaged in the moment, enjoying the thrill of just being.

The art of riding untangles the threads that wrap around the brain, that obscure the past and bind up the future. Riding brings the mind front and center into the moment to experience the ultimate now. Welcome to the adventure, free from yesterday and tomorrow, free from the ego of knowing all. Welcome to the true path.

How are we to blossom, sprout, grow, evolve? How are we to do that if we don't take the risk to seed something new that will take root in the fertile ground of our hearts? A passion that takes root is the bloom of our truth.

Riding is an act of faith. It takes courage to venture beyond a mirage of comfort and free our adventuresome dreams to take root. So, grab life by the handlebars! Get wild! Get free! Good girls go further than bad girls, and that makes a good girl bad to the bone, the real definition of a bad ass. Saddle up and explore the wide open. Everybody can get on their own highway. God will take you places you've never been before and will show you some very fun times along the way, as long as you show up and let truth fuel you. The loudest voice in the wind is the loving spirit of encouragement.

The Chrome Cowgirl spirit is about sticking to your guns and letting your free spirit soar, not sour. You're your own cowpoke, my friends. Get out there and weather those storms and ride unfamiliar roads; that is where things will make sense. You'll be living and riding a new trail, blazed and ordained by your deepest desires come true.

In the movie *Shawshank Redemption,* Morgan Freeman said: "Either get busy livin' or get busy dyin'." To me, that sounds a lot like "shut up and ride." Get busy riding or get busy sighing about there being more to life. Everyone out there would benefit from a little rev of the throttle to make her (or his) soul roar to life! Always remember, you're fiercely gorgeous; you're a revolutionary; you're a blossom; you have mental toughness; you're a rebel with applause! Saddle up and . . . ride 'em Chrome Cowgirl!

Sasha xo

My Journey is going to take me right on past your Destination..!

Rest In Peace
SAMANTHA MORGAN
2008

"Motorcycles are my life. It's like breathing. When I go up on the wall, I ride by the odds. I try to keep my odds down. It's like drawing. When you create something, it comes from within; nobody can ever take that away from you. Everything you do up on the wall is all yours. There happens to be extra adrenaline there (goes with the G-force), as well as a mental discipline, which makes one stronger. It's a gift."

— *Samantha Morgan, MotorDrome trick rider; inductee, Sturgis Motorcycle Hall of Fame 2006*
(excerpt from Bikerlady: Living & Riding Free*)*

Samantha will forever be a pioneer in the world of women in motorcycling. Her beautiful wonder-filled personality ignited the light in all of our souls when we watched her racing around inside the wooden barrel of the American MotorDrome Company's "Wall of Death." Sam liked to refer to it as the "Thrillarena." And thrills were what you'd experience seeing Sam soaring around inside the cylinder. Sonny Pelaquin was her mentor who took the teen orphan into his family and became a father to her. "He gave me my great life and taught me how to be a trick rider and showman." Sam rode in some eleven Dromes worldwide.

Oh how I loved to visit with Sammy-girl at the M Drome. She brought out the little-girl excitement in me as I would lean my arm out over the rail, excitedly waiting for her to snatch that dollar bill from my grip as she raced by riding with no hands, laughing as she collected the waving Lincoln and Washington faces rippling in the G-force wind. Her smile was comforting, and our conversations were always filled with girlie giggles as we spoke in dreamy concepts about anything in life. We fawned about our deep passion for riding and how our motorcycles were our means to living and riding free. Sam, you are so deeply missed by all of us. We love you and will keep your memory alive. You are a hero and a rollin' role model to us all.

Samantha Morgan: A hero and role model to us all. *Sara Liberte*

APPENDIX

INTERNET RESOURCES: CYBERCHROME COWGIRLS

* Christine Firehock: www.christineskickstart.com
* Ellen Reid Smith: www.cowgirlsmarts.com
* DJ Jones: www.poseyfoundation.com
* Dawn Norakas: www.stingercustomcycles.com
* JoAnn Bortles: www.crazyhorsepainting.com
* Erika Lopez: www.erikalopez.com
* Sara Liberte: www.saraliberte.com
* Sarah Lyon: www.sarahlyon.com
* Nika Rolczewski: www.racerchicks.com
* Laura Klock: www.kustomcycles.com
* Betsy Huelskamp: www.betsyhuelskamp.com
* Athena: www.vagabondchoppers.com
* Chopper Chick Crew: www.chopperchicks.com
* Vivian "Gypsy" Charros: www.gypsyhighwaycustom.com
* Mandie Crawford: www.roaringwomen.com
* Cycle Sisters MC, Bonnie Frankel: www.cyclesistersmc.com
* Christabel Zamor: www.hoopgirl.com
* Vicki Gray: www.motoress.com
* Valerie Thompson: www.vtracegirl.com
* Marjorie Kleiman: www.myspace.com/njbikergrrrl
* Jasmine Cain: www.myspace.com/jasminecain
* Genevieve Schmitt: www.womanridersnow.com
* Samantha Morgan: www.thrillarena.com
* Pepper Massey: www.sturgismotorcyclerally.com

FUNDRAISER EVENTS

* www.womensmotorcyclistfoundation.org—Pony Express Ride to benefit Susan G. Komen Cancer Foundation
* www.ladylibertyride.com—Ride to benefit L.O.V.E., Leave Out Violence, ending violence youth to youth

MOTORCYCLE WEBSITES AND OTHER RESOURCES
* www.lonelyplanet.com
* www.whitehorsepress.com
* www.motorbooks.com
* www.horizonsunlimited.com
* www.madmaps.com
* www.motorcyclemisadventures.com

COOL BIKER CHICK 'ZINES
* www.motoress.com
* www.helmethair.com
* www.bikerally.com
* www.vtwinmama.com
* www.womenridersnow.com
* www.roadrunner.travel
* www.womenx.com
* www.frictionzone.com

COOL CHROME COWBOY WEBSITES
* www.bikernet.com
* www.cyrilhuze.com
* www.cyclesource.com
* www.lichterphoto.com
* www.strokersdallas.com
* www.tropicaltattoo.com
* www.beanre.com
* www.delavegainternational.com

GET YER MOTOR REVVIN': RIDER TRAINING WEBSITES
* MSF Motorcycle Safety Foundation: www.msf-usa.org
* Rider's Edge: www.ridersedge.com
* Ride Like a Pro: www.ridelikeapro.com
* Christine's KickSTART Motorcycle Training Series: www.christineskickstart.com
* Keith Code's Twist of the Wrist DVD: www.superbikeschool.com
* MSF Dirt Bike School: www.dirtbikeschool.com

SHUT UP AND SADDLE UP! Visit www.chromecowgirl.com for lots more goodies.

INDEX